Customer Relationship Marketing

GET TO KNOW YOUR CUSTOMERS AND WIN THEIR LOYALTY

MERLIN STONE, NEIL WOODCOCK AND LIZ MACHTYNGER

IN ASSOCIATION WITH

Marketing MAGAZINE

KOGAN PAGE

C000078651

DEDICATIONS

To Ofra – thanks for keeping me on the right track and preventing me from being an even worse workaholic!   *Merlin*

To Julia, Callum, Aliya, Mum and Dad – always supportive.   *Neil*

To Jon, Mum and Dad – thank you for your love, support and challenge!   *Liz*

First published in 1995
Second edition published 2000

Apart from any fair dealing for the purposes of research or private study, or criticism or review, as permitted under the Copyright, Designs and Patents Act 1988, this publication may only be reproduced, stored or transmitted, in any form or by any means, with the prior permission in writing of the publishers, or in the case of reprographic reproduction in accordance with the terms and licences issued by the CLA. Enquiries concerning reproduction outside these terms should be sent to the publishers at the undermentioned addresses:

Kogan Page Limited
120 Pentonville Road
London
N1 9JN
UK

Kogan Page Limited
163 Central Avenue, Suite 4
Dover
NH 03820
USA

© Merlin Stone, Neil Woodcock and Liz Machtynger, 2000

The rights of Merlin Stone, Neil Woodcock and Liz Machtynger to be identified as the authors of this work have been asserted by them in accordance with the Copyright, Designs and Patents Act 1988.

British Library Cataloguing in Publication Data

A CIP record for this book is available from the British Library.

ISBN 0 7494 2700 0

Typeset by Jean Cussons Typesetting, Diss, Norfolk
Printed and bound in Great Britain by Clays Ltd, St Ives plc

Contents

Acknowledgements

It's now about 15 years since Mike Wallbridge invited me to help British Telecom (as it was then) move into the (then) esoteric world of database marketing, and Mike and BT continue to influence my thinking. The various worlds in which I have worked – database marketing, customer service, marketing of IT, key account management – came together in relationship marketing, then customer relationship marketing, then customer relationship management and so on. So, I owe much to clients and friends (the categories aren't mutually exclusive!) from all these worlds. They include Alison Bond of AB Associates, Wanda Goldwag of Air Miles, Janet Davies of American Express, Jes Jarvis of Arjo Wiggins, David Backinsell, Julian Berry and Barry Leventhal of Berry Consulting, Peter Cook and Catherine Macleod-Smith of BP, Sally Martyn of BKM Ogilvy One, Mark Patron of Claritas, Phil Dourado and Sheelagh Mundell of Customer Service Management, Russell Bowman and Yvonne Graves of British Airways, Bill George of Customer Loyalty 2000, Steven Georgiadis of Direct Line, Jeanna Gdulin of EDS, Tess Harris of Elektra Associates, John Grey of Equifax, Amanda Arthur of Evans Hunt Scott, Catherine Gale of Grey Worldwide, Ruth Rowan of Henry Stewart Conference Studies, Daryn Moody of Henry Stewart Publications, Wendy Hewson of Hewson Group, Cliff Hudson of Homebase, Professor Derek Holder of the Institute of Direct Marketing, Liz Harlow and Alan Jelly of the Jigsaw Consortium, Derek Davies of Kingston University, Linda Jakab of Mercantile

Mutual, Charles Arthur, Executive Director of Miller Freeman Direct, John Adcock, Martin Hickley and Martin Schoelkmann of Mummert + Partner, Doug Houston of NatWest, Bill Savage and Stuart Lamb of Norwich Union, Dave Hudson of Old Mutual, John Fletcher of Orange, Peter Bartram and Chris Butler of Policy Publications, Paul Rayfield, Paul Weston and David Williams of QCi, Jon Epstein of Results 'R' Us, Peter Lavers of Rolls-Royce, Mark Garratt of Royal & Sun Alliance, Iain Henderson and David Loble of Royal Mail, Stephanie Penning and Nigel Armstead of the SAS Institute, Bob Shaw of Shaw International, Lucy Jacobs of Siebel, Tony Woods of Statistical Applications, Professor Paul Gamble and Professor Peter Kangis of Surrey European Management School, University of Surrey, Dave Cox, Andy Hunter and Steve Quigley of Swallow Information Systems, Peter Phelan and Wanda Warhaftig of Swiss Re, Joe Stephenson of UPS, Gerard Ingram of VW-Gedas, Peter Wray of Wray Associates, Ian Law and Andy Poole of Yorkshire Electricity. All the members of my customer management group – who include most of the above – have, of course, been very helpful.

At IBM, many colleagues have helped me over the years. They include – in the UK – Edward Ben-nathan, Adrian Bird, Steve Byrne, Mark Cerasale, Kevin Condron, Colin Devonport, Bryan Foss, Ron Hulman, Richard Lowrie, Fariba Mclurcan, Alla Main, John Mullaly, Jonathan Miller, Arthur Parker, Gill Whitelegg. In Australia they include Scott Barlow, Dorothy Beagley, Emma Black, Nerida Caesar, John Cutterham, John Garrett, Victor Grasty, Doug Morrison, Ian Mulligan, Paul Robinson, Libby Webster. In the US they include Ben Barnes, Vince Jones, Ginny Rometty, Brian Scheld and Harvey Thompson. In Israel they include Osnat Dror and Osnat Segev.

Naturally, it's not just individuals who have influenced me, but also the companies they work for. I've learned most by working with companies such as Acxiom, BP, BT, British Airways, Citroën, Equifax, Mercantile Mutual, Microstrategy, Norwich Union, Royal & Sun Alliance, Sainsbury's, Homebase, Siebel, Unilever, Vauxhall, UPS, Volkswagen, Wiggins Teape, Yorkshire Electricity and, of course, my sponsors IBM, where ideas on customer management dovetail so closely with mine.

Merlin Stone

There is no such thing as a new idea, only new syntheses of old ones. Our work in global account management, customer service, customer relationship management and IT often involves rearranging old concepts and shaping them so that they become more usable and effective in complicated organizations. There are many people and companies who help me do this and who provide much of the inspiration behind the ideas and themes in this book. It is always difficult to single out individuals, but thanks in particular to Anne Gowan from *The Daily Telegraph*, Jo Gibbs, Mike Nash and Ian Sanderson from BP Amoco Chemicals, Doug Houston from NatWest, Iain Henderson, Chris Powell and Dave Chapman from The Post Office, Berndt Zierhut from BP Retail, David Hudson from Britannic Assurance, John Furmston from BT, Robin Mitchell from Lorien, Tony Slater and Roseleen Donohue (formerly) from Barclays Merchant Services, Melanie Howard from the Future Foundation, Derek Holder from the Institute of Direct Marketing and Peter Georgeu, Managing Director of Direct Access, SA – they have all contributed significantly to my understanding of what managing customers is really about. Also, thanks to those people we are working with at IBM, NCR, Wunderman Cato Johnson and others on customer management assessment projects around the world. The insights from these projects enable us to keep some sort of grip on reality.

Finally, I'd like to thank my fellow directors at QCi; Paul Weston, Paul Rayfield and David Williams for their intelligence, vision, practical common sense, tenacity, humour, energy, undying optimism and, last but not least, patience. It's great working with you!

Neil Woodcock

The greatest stimulus for ideas creation for me has come from experiences in actively managing customers and working with people passionate about this area! I would like to thank a few of these people in particular.

My long-suffering colleagues with whom I initiated the Customer Management Programme for BP Oil Europe back in 1990, especially Catherine Macleod-Smith, Ashkan Samimi-Mofakam, Penny Ouvry, Mike Tunstall and Mike Boda.

Bryan Foss, Martin Hickley, Mike Wallbridge and Dave Snowden, above all, for their challenging and forward-thinking ideas on customer knowledge management.

My customers and colleagues, who have really made, and are continuing to make, a difference in the implementation of customer management. In particular, Iain Robson, Adrian Brown, Keith Carter, Mark Garratt, Todd Cini, Graeme Sherrington, Rob Strange, Bill Savage, Gaynor Phillips and John Adcock.

Those organizations daring enough to want to put customers and knowledge first, specifically BP, Royal & Sun Alliance, Norwich Union, Mummert + Partner and Legal & General.

Finally, to those people who really provided a new context and confidence to my ideas and work during my MBA programme. In particular, Ronnie Lessem, Sudhanshu Palsule, Mick May, Neal Cavalier-Smith, Alan Clark and Boyd Rodger.

Liz Machtynger

Preface

It is now over five years since we started work on the first edition of this book. In the time since then, many things have changed and many things have stayed the same. In the area of relationship marketing, the major areas of change have been in the terminology. Customer relationship marketing, or CRM, is now the accepted term in learning how to implement better customer management and systems that enable this to occur. It is in these areas that we have added new material. However, the principles of managing relationships with customers have remained the same, with one exception – in many situations, customers can use information and communications technology to manage companies, rather than the other way round.

The other thing that has changed for us, the authors, is the enormous amount of experience that we have gained in this area. We have not only been consulting in this area, but also researching intensely. Our more advanced findings have been published in several ways. *Up Close and Personal: CRM @ Work* (Kogan Page, 1999), written by Paul Gamble, Merlin Stone and Neil Woodcock, makes an important contribution to CRM knowledge. The IBM series of briefings – 'Close to the Customer' – continues to be published by Policy Publications several times a year, with sponsors as diverse as IBM, Equifax, Royal Mail and UPS. It is the research for this series that has provided us with the new material in this edition (in Chapters 1, 2, 13 and 14). However, the rest of the book is largely still valid, updated as necessary to reflect the impacts of new technology and changing definitions. Two of the original chapters have been deleted. The chapter on databases has gone – not because it was irrelevant, but because we have replaced it with a much broader chapter on CRM systems. The same applies to the original chapter on campaign management and the media. The basics of both these are covered in many good books on direct marketing, such as Merlin Stone, Derek Davies and Alison Bond's *Direct Hit* (Pitman, 1995). We have also deleted the original final chapter on capability development, incorporating the information in *Up Close and Personal*.

Foreword

When the first edition of this book was published in 1995, customer relationship marketing, or CRM, was a relatively new discipline that had freshly emerged from a quality-oriented combination of database marketing, account management and customer service. It was apparent even then how critically the new discipline depended on information technology for its success. It was also evident that well-planned, sensible deployment of information technology would be key to increasing profitability through CRM – a lesson that many companies have learnt the hard way.

However, what few people foresaw back in 1995 was how much change was still yet to happen in information technology, particularly where managing customers was concerned. Today, the rapid growth of the World Wide Web and the emergence of the mobile telephone as a customer communication technology means that corporations making plans for their future customer management have far more ways of managing customers – and, indeed, letting their customers manage them.

Just as importantly, there have been immense advances in our ability to capture, make sense of and deploy the vast increase in the information flowing up and down the value chain, particularly between customers and their suppliers. Combined with the new customer-interface technologies, corporations can now automatically customize their offerings to the very latest needs of customers, which have been expressed during the customers' latest interactions with the corporation. This can take place in less than a second. The vision of 'my company' has been made a reality. Similarly, corporations can decide which of their customers are worth managing – and which are not – with much greater certainty. Good customers can be identified and a forecast made of their behaviour. Bad customers can be detected and their possible damage to the corporation can be limited. On a more positive note, customers can obtain information about products, services and their relationships with their suppliers far more easily.

In the world of financial services – whether banking or insurance, and whether for businesses or consumers – the take-up of new technology for managing customers has been very rapid. The technology can be used to:

■ increase market share;
■ reduce the costs of customer management;
■ recruit new, high-quality customers in a more targeted fashion;
■ defend and retain existing customers;
■ develop more value out of existing customers;
■ protect companies against riskier customers.

For new entrants, the new technologies have provided ideal attack tools, enabling them to pick the most profitable customers or existing players, and provide them with unparalleled levels of service; levels that would once only have been possible through major investments in bricks rather than clicks. In terms of how markets work, the new technologies have allowed totally different models of customer management to emerge, such as spot-buying and auctioning. Many of these seem the complete antithesis of CRM, and they only work because they meet customers' needs, but the foundations of CRM remain the same.

This second edition has been extensively updated due to the impact of technologies and the new models of customer management they make possible, but it also remains faithful to the practical and quality-oriented view of the first edition. Corporations still need to do their research and analysis to identify which customers are worth managing, using which model – plus, of course, which customers want to be managed in different ways.

Corporations still need to get their people, processes and systems in order if they are to deliver customer management to the quality they promise their customers – and do it cost-effectively.

Corporations still need to measure what they are doing, and check that they are delivering what they promised. New and well-established technologies must still be deployed carefully to be able to bring returns to the corporation, while still satisfying the customer.

Jerry Cole, General Manager, IBM Global Financial Services Sector
Michael P. Haydock, Vice President, IBM Business Intelligence
Consulting & Services

February 2000

1

Why Relationship Marketing?

As with many management fashions, relationship marketing, customer relationship marketing and relationship management are terms that many managers or marketers use but define in different ways. When we wrote the first edition of this book in 1995, the term relationship marketing was commonly used. Today, the set of ideas that we use to improve customer management has passed through different phases, including:

- customer relationship marketing, which included a very strong focus on the customer;
- customer relationship management, which was supposed to remedy the alleged neglect of other functions' contributions to the management of customer relationships;
- enterprise relationship marketing, which adds the supply chain dimension;
- e-CRM – electronic customer relationship management – which adds the focus of e-business.

However, despite these changes, the fundamental focus of the activities described by these changing names has remained the same, in line with our early definition of relationship marketing, which was – and still is:

The use of a wide range of marketing, sales, communication, service and customer care approaches to:

- identify a company's named individual customers;
- create a relationship between the company and its customers that stretches over many transactions;
- manage that relationship to the benefit of the customers and the company.

The additional aspects referred to in the above definitions have certainly developed beyond our original concepts, so we have covered them fully in our more advanced book, *Up Close and Personal: CRM @ Work* (Gamble, P, Stone, M and Woodcock, N, 1999, Kogan Page, London).

Our original definition, while technically a good one, is a little lacking in feeling. In marketing, a good way to define a concept or technique is in terms of what we want our customers to think or feel as a result of us using it, one we could even explain to customers. So a company could describe relationship marketing to its customers as below.

Relationship marketing is how we:

- find you;
- get to know you;
- keep in touch with you;
- try to ensure that you get what you want from us in every aspect of our dealings with you;
- check that you are getting what we promised you

… subject, of course, to it being worth while to us as well.

In the late 1990s, relationship marketing became a heady fashion among managers of marketing, service and information technology, and even general managers. This was despite strong evidence that many consumers did not want to be managed in relationships and that, in industrial markets, many big buyers used their relationships with suppliers to extract maximum value while returning minimum value. We are therefore cautious about over-using the word relationship – we only use it where we feel that it is justified, except when we use the standard term 'relationship marketing'. However, customers can be managed in many ways – the theme of Chapter 2 of this book. Relationship marketing – or customer relationship marketing (CRM) as we refer to it in the rest of this book – is just one of the possible models of customer management. In many situations, we prefer to use the term customer management (CM), because it does not imply a particular model of customer management.

MANAGING THE RELATIONSHIP IN STAGES

In markets in which buyers and sellers experience benefits from developing relationships, these are rarely simple relationships in which a customer is 100 per cent loyal to one company or to another. Most relationships develop in stages, with customers sampling different products and often remaining 'switchers' or 'multi-sourcers' – buying from several companies. To help companies manage this situation, we have developed a simple model of relationship development. Many companies have used it to understand their customers better and develop policies for improving the relationship. We summarize the relationship as a series of stages, and then identify how many customers are at each stage and what takes them to the next stage. In Figure 1.1, we explain these stages, their definitions and the problems some companies have in managing them.

We would like to see some recognition that:

▓ customers don't simply move from being 'prospects' to 100 per cent 'loyal customers' and then to 'lost customers';
▓ stages of the relationship can be identified and managed;
▓ data can be used to manage this activity.

WHY CRM IS IMPORTANT

CRM is important because acquiring customers is usually much more expensive than keeping them.

This is most obvious in direct marketing, where the costs of acquiring and keeping customers can be accurately quantified. In other marketing environments, estimates show that the same is

Stage	Definition	Typical problems and opportunities
Targeting	When the customer is targeted as being an appropriate customer for the company, and induced to 'join'.	Targeting is not precise enough. So, if the company tries to cross-sell to all its existing customers, irrespective of their suitability, this can be a loss-making activity. Very large numbers of customers are targeted, using a variety of approaches – direct mail, off the page, TV. This leads to overlapping coverage and wasted promotional budgets. At worst, if the activities of different product managers are not coordinated, the same person may be targeted for several different products at the same time, with the same names being rented more than once.
Enquiry management	The customer is in the process of joining.	Usually a very short stage, but of critical importance. In many cases, failure to manage enquiries properly leads to many customers being lost before they join. Sometimes this process is just too expensive compared with subsequent customer value. At this stage, customers' expectations are often set for future treatment, yet they are often disappointed.
Welcoming	After the customer has joined, depending on the complexity of the product or service, it is important to ensure that the customer is 'securely on board', eg knows who to contact if there are problems, knows how to use the product or service.	This is also often a very short stage, yet it is clear from what happens when a customer has problems or makes a claim that they often do not know who to call or what to do. For decisions involving significant outlays, customers may need to be reassured that they have made the correct decision and given the opportunity to say whether or not they feel they could have been handled better during the buying cycle.
Getting to know	This is a crucial period, when both sides exchange information with each other. Additional customers' needs may become apparent and how they use the product or	Many companies assume that this stage does not exist and that their customers go straight into a mature state of account management. Yet, if we take the example of financial services, the early cancellations that occur with many types of insurance policies and loans indicate that this is

Stage	Definition	Typical problems and opportunities
	service becomes known. More is also learnt about customers' honesty, ability to pay and so on.	clearly not so. We cannot expect that no customers will cancel early, but we can expect to be able, by means of data analysis, to identify customers most likely to and implement preventive action. Experience in insurance and banking shows that if we try, we will have some success. Analysis of other industries with long-term relationships with customers indicates that communications behaviour, brand attitudes and satisfaction with the category are good predictors of loyalty. Strong preferences can be formed quite early on in the relationship, eg if they respond to your communications, rate your brand highly and are satisfied with how you have arranged their portfolio of products or services, then they will be more likely to stay with you.
Customer development	The relationship is now being managed securely, with additional needs being identified in time and met where feasible.	This is the ideal state, though quite a few customers never reach it and often dip into the next stage or remain in the previous stage for a long time. This is best detected by short questionnaires, which can be administered by mail, telephone or by sales staff.
Managing problems	Customers can have such severe problems that special attention is needed to ensure that they return safely to customer development. If this attention is not given, customers can be so dissatisfied that divorce is imminent. If customers do leave, they will usually, after a cooling-off period, be ready for 'winback'.	This stage is defined in terms of what suppliers should do, but, of course, the need for it is often missed and customers go straight into pre-divorce, eg after a mishandled service event or a change in their needs that remains undetected. If a company does not handle the initial problem well, and customers consider leaving, companies often fail to recognize that this is happening. Surprisingly, many companies give up here, and even pride themselves that they make it easy for customers to cancel. If the reason for cancellation or termination of the relationship was a change in circumstances or a move out of the category, then brand loyalty may be intact and, in some cases, enhanced if suppliers made termination easy.

Stage	Definition	Typical problems and opportunities
Winback	Sometimes, the relationship ended because of high price or the wrong product, so winback can be initiated when these issues are resolved. Winback is hardest if customers left due to poor service, unless competitors' service is even worse!	The targeting of winback campaigns is made difficult because many companies are poor at defining and identifying lost customers and they have no reliable customer database.

Figure 1.1 *Stages in managing the customer relationship*

true. The benefits of CRM can be shown by means of accounting techniques that reveal:

■ costs of acquiring customers;
■ changes in the number of customers;
■ changes in what each customer is buying.

The benefits of CRM are usually in one or more of these areas:

■ improved customer retention and loyalty – customers stay longer, buy more, more often – that is, increased long-term value;
■ higher customer profitability, not just because each customer buys more, but because of lower costs of recruiting customers and no need to recruit so many to maintain a steady volume of business;
■ reduced cost of sales, as existing customers are usually more responsive.

However, acquiring the wrong customers and keeping them is often very damaging. Focusing on customer retention as a top business priority can be very stupid if most customers are not profitable. In many industries – such as banking, general insurance and utilities, and also in many business-to-business situations – a significant proportion of customers are unprofitable, because the cost to serve them is much higher than the benefit derived from them. In such situations, customer management techniques are best deployed to reduce the costs of serving them or even get rid of unprofitable customers.

From the customers' viewpoint, research across many sectors in both business and consumer markets shows repeatedly that customers' most important requirements are clear and understandable. They can be summarized by the following statements:

- 'When I enquire about the product, give me advice promptly and courteously and do the things that you say you will do when you say you will do them.'
- 'Be timely and relevant in your contacts with me.'
- 'Make it easy for me to contact you.'
- 'Make it easy for me to buy the product I want at a competitive price. I want the product to be complete and working, and if the product is being delivered, for it to be delivered as specified, on time and in full.'
- 'Use the data I give you properly and ethically and in ways that benefit me, and make sure you can access it when I am in contact with you.'
- 'After the sale, don't pester me, but keep in touch if there is something to say. More importantly, if I have a problem or ask for support, please give it promptly and courteously.'
- 'Trust me and live up to your promises.'

To meet these requirements it is necessary to put in place:

- good manufacturing/operations and distribution;
- properly recruited, trained and motivated people;
- robust enquiry, welcoming, sales and complaints-handling processes and measurement systems;
- good information technology, so that the company can recognize customers and provide relevant offers, information and advice.

These customer requirements should be translated into basic business practices. In the majority of large corporations, however, they are not.

If your proposition matches customers' requirements and you are friendly and professional in the way you deal with them at all stages, the benefits are massive. Our research shows that if you align your customer management with customers' needs, you will:

- reduce your customer loss rate by at least 25 per cent – one in four customers is lost for simple service reasons, not serious service errors; three in four you will lose anyway for reasons that are out of your control, such as the customers' needs changing so that they no longer need your product or service;
- hold on to customers longer – this is linked to the above point, but, of course, becomes a different revenue line on a business case (there are too many variations here to give an average figure);
- maintain or even improve margins with existing customers because the strength of your relationship with them results in their being more resistant to aggressive competitive pricing;
- improve your penetration rate and share of spend, often increasing your share of target customers' business by tens of percentage points;
- apart from an increase in referred business, there will be an impact here too in that your core business acquisition processes (targeting and enquiry management) will be professional and robust – this alone will increase your new business, sometimes significantly.

THE FIVE KEY ELEMENTS OF CUSTOMER MANAGEMENT

In all our work, a common theme has been that success in managing customers depends partly on applying some standard general management principles. We believe that this point is often missed. These principles can be summarized as follows (see Figure 1.2).

Models of customer management

Consider the different models that apply to the domain in which you are considering implementing customer management. Consider how these models may be combined, and how they will evolve. This is the subject of Chapter 2.

Customer management strategy/strategies
Which customers to manage, via which channels, with
which business partners, with what business results, in
terms of benefits to customers and company?
NB: *Strategies are likely to be subject to change in a*
changing business environment, particularly if there is
activity in areas such as merger, acquisition, partnership,
deregulation, privatization.

Customer management model(s)
The overall processes by means of which customers are
recruited, retained and developed. These include classic
CRM, customized communication, spot-selling, etc.
NB: *These models ensure that the strategy and its benefits*
are deliverable. They are often combined. However,
particular models may remain virtually unchanged while
customer management strategies change.

Customer management infrastructure
The systems, data, detailed processes and measures that
enable customer management models to achieve
particular strategies.
NB: *These may be constant across more than one model*
and more than one strategy (eg customer data
warehouse, Web-enabled buying, customer contact
measurement, customer management assessment
method).

People
How staff members are recruited, trained, organized,
managed, motivated and rewarded to deploy the
infrastructure and work within customer management
models to achieve customer management strategies.
NB: *This includes customer knowledge management,*
although some of this may be transferred completely to
systems, to allow lower-cost staff to be used or to replace
them completely.

Customer management programme
A programme of projects for implementing customer
management, structured to allow simultaneous creation,
implementation and management of the customer
management approach.
NB: *This is best described as a programme for 'changing*
the engines in flight', as it involves developing and testing
strategies and models, installing and using the
infrastructure, while trying to get business results. It
therefore requires tough programme management
disciplines.

Figure 1.2   *The five key elements of customer management*

Customer management strategy

This determines which customers you want to manage, when and by means of which channels. It is intimately connected with the decision as to which models of customer management you wish to use.

Systems, data and processes

Determine how your chosen model(s) need to be supported by systems, data and processes. Recognize that these, too, will evolve as your model of customer management evolves. This implies:

■ systems that are not designed to be the solution that ends all solutions, but, rather, ones that are more flexible, communicating with and updating each other using middleware;
■ data that improves in quality, but may also change in scope;
■ processes that improve over time and are, where possible, self-improving, as you come to understand more about how your supply chain works to meet the needs of your intermediate and end-customers.

People

Although the proportion of value-added contributed by *people* – as opposed to electronically – is likely to be in decline, people will still be involved in planning and implementation. Different skill sets and motivation may be required, implying different approaches to recruitment, training and line management.

Customer management programme

This is your programme of change – a series of projects that implement your new approach in different domains, for different purposes, at different stages of the relationship cycle. Recognize that this programme will continue to change as you make progress in implementing e-business. In general, we recommend that detailed planning for more than a year ahead may be inappropriate, so an outline plan for the second and subsequent years may be more appropriate.

In this book, we show you how to do all these things, and also the pitfalls to avoid.

2

Models of Customer Management

There is no single model of customer management that works in every market. Marketers have been brought up on models such as consumer goods branding, retail marketing and salesforce management. Then along comes CRM, claiming to replace, or substantially supplement, these tried and tested ways of doing business. Is it worth all the work involved in changing things? One of the major factors that has influenced our thinking on this question is the rapid change in customer behaviour that has been prompted by new marketing technologies – typically direct marketing technologies such as telemarketing and, latterly, the World Wide Web. Let us examine what these models are and how they work.

The main paradigms that we have identified are listed below. Note that, in practice, the way many companies do their marketing is a combination of these.

CUSTOMER RELATIONSHIP MARKETING (CRM)

CRM is still the aspiration of most companies. In practice, most companies make much slower progress than they would like, but get solid gains by prioritizing those areas of the relationship where the offer for target (such as positive and/or high-value) customers is most at variance with the need. This model recognizes that the relationship is only one part of the marketing mix, and that there are often situations where classic elements of the *market* mix are the more critical requirements for marketing success (leadership in terms of product, price, brand, retail location and so on, for example).

Interestingly, this model originated in best practice in business-to-business marketing – a combination of account management and customer service. We have found that even for companies that want no truck with final customer CRM, it works very well when managing intermediaries. The difference is that in trade marketing, the determinants of customer loyalty tend to be very different from those of consumer marketing. In trade marketing, the product offer is largely taken for granted – if the product does not meet the needs of intermediaries' customers, then it will not be resold by them. In our work on customer loyalty (Stone, M et al, 1998, *Customer Loyalty: Best practice*, Policy Publications), we outlined the general determinants of customer loyalty. The determinants of business-to-business customer loyalty tend to be:

■ satisfaction with brand and category;
■ service experience and satisfaction;
■ offer attunement – whether or not the supplier will modify the offer to meet the customer's specific needs;
■ involvement in the design/delivery process – the more complicated and advanced the product, the more important this is;
■ good relationship management;
■ balance of selling and buying facilitation – that is, a combination of push and pull – customers do expect push from suppliers with good products;
■ information exchange.

The balance of factors depends on:

■ company type/size/sector;
■ product/service type;
■ importance of product/service to them and their customers – whether the business customer is an intermediary or the next level in the value chain;
■ nature of/criteria for the buying decision;

■ attitude to business relationships, including relationships with their own customers.

Where trade loyalty is concerned, the basic motivations are the same as in business-to-business relationships, but different marketing mix elements are used to achieve that loyalty. They can usually be split into hygiene factors, which are those that, if they were lacking, the supplier would not even be considered, and loyalty factors, which determine how much of the intermediary's business the supplier gets.

Hygiene factors tend to be the classic marketing mix variables, such as:

■ product
■ price
■ margin
■ packaging
■ advertising.

Loyalty factors tend to include:

■ delivery timing and accuracy;
■ stock availability;
■ invoicing;
■ information for them and their customers;
■ query handling;
■ effective promotional support.

Notice that this is more or less the reverse of hygiene and loyalty factors in consumer markets. Put more informally, a loyal trade customer is one that trusts that:

■ the supplier's product will sell well;
■ customers will continue to be satisfied with the supplier's product and continue to buy it again and again;
■ consumers will only come back to compliment, not complain;
■ the supplier has targeted its consumers correctly (promotionally and in terms of product design).

All the above help define the relationship offer. If the offer is good, then classic CRM can be applied. This follows the principles outlined in our previous works on CRM strategy and implementation (Stone, M et al, 1997, *Relationship Marketing Strategy*, Policy Publications and Stone, M et al, 1997, *Building Customer Relationships: Best Practice*, Policy Publications). These include the following elements in particular:

■ identifying those intermediaries most receptive to the relationship offer;
■ identifying current and potential value;
■ managing intermediaries by contact channels/frequencies that correlate with their current and expected future value, identifying when there are problems in the relationship cycle.

In addition, because many intermediaries are small businesses, with particular susceptibility to bad debt and fraud, it helps to follow the techniques for managing good and bad customers as per our work on customer-focused data (Stone, M et al, 1998, *Building Customer-focused Data*, Policy Publications).

ONE TO ONE

This is D Peppers and M Rogers' ideal (1997, *Enterprise One-to-One*, Doubleday). Here, as far as possible, most aspects of the marketing mix are actively attuned to the (changing) individual, based on information given by them before or during contacts, perhaps supplemented by other data about them (such as that which can be inferred). They reject the idea of the segment of one, as this is seen as static. Some (but not all) customers are seen to be very receptive to this – that is, it is acknowledged that customers have different propensities to respond in terms of returning more value.

In general, the returns for the enormous systems and data investments required to achieve this are not clear and reliable, though there are some good examples of success. These usually occur when the principle is applied to large customers, whose value justifies the degree of customization involved in this approach. In fact, in many cases, this applies to the relationship between large suppliers and large intermediaries. For example, the link between a grocery food company, such as Unilever or Procter & Gamble, and large retailers, such as Wall-Mart, Tesco or

Carrefour, is probably the nearest to an intermediary one-to-one relationship. Although the products supplied are normally standard, the rest of the offer (payment terms, delivery, information and so on) is usually heavily customized.

TRANSPARENT MARKETING

This is our own idea, which is that many customers would like to manage their relationships with companies rather than the other way round (Stone, M et al, 1998, The future of relationship marketing – towards transparent marketing?, *Journal of Database Marketing*, 6 (1), pp 11–23). Customers would like to do this by soliciting information from them, customizing the offer made to them (regarding content, timing and other such details), but they are not usually allowed to do so. However, where this is possible (for example, via advanced call centres or the Web), some customers are very responsive to it. However, most companies do not offer anything like this to their customers. Instead, they often waste a lot of money trying to guess what customers want, based on inadequate information.

Interestingly, one of the major successes in the deployment of the Web is in providing transparent marketing to intermediaries. The Web enables intermediaries to access their suppliers' order processing and delivery systems, customize their requirements, track the supply process and the like. Many insurance companies have found that insurance brokers have taken up their Web-based customer management offers very quickly. In the automotive industry, those companies that have allowed customers on-line access to product specification systems have experienced the same effect. This on-line access may be provided at dealer sites or else on the Web. In our work on customer management in the automotive industry (Stone, M et al, 1998, *Managing Automotive Customers*, Policy Publications and Stone, M et al, 1999, *Best Practice Customer Management*, Policy Publications), we showed how leading motor manufacturers in the United States were organizing their intermediaries to provide browsable best-price offers on the Web. Notice that this does not detract from the value added by resellers – advice, allowing inspection and test-driving of the car and so on.

PERSONALIZING OF COMMUNICATIONS AND STANDARD OFFERS

This is very common and has grown out of good practice in direct mail and telemarketing. It is used especially for campaign selection and packaging of the offer. It involves good use of available data (including that previously given by customers) and good data-quality management. It can lead to substantial uplifts in response and conversion rates and significant savings in communication costs (particularly outbound). It may involve tens, hundreds or even thousands of cells in a large outbound mail campaign, in which the offer made to each customer is selected from one of many (often modular) offers, according to the customers' profiles, and presented to each customer using personalization. In its most advanced form, data given by the customer at the point of contact is used to create or modify the profile and, hence, the offer made.

Interestingly, these principles have been shown to apply just as well to intermediary marketing, where there are very large numbers of small intermediaries, whose behaviour in terms of responsiveness to communication is similar to that of consumers – that is, they tend to take action when prompted.

This is also manageable via intermediaries – especially in situations in which the channel is an administered one. The motor industry is perhaps the best example, where the supplier and dealer collect data jointly, and the customer receives personalized mailings sent by the supplier on behalf of the dealer, inviting the customer to view the latest model, replace his or her car, come in for service or other offer. Another example is where a retailer works with a financial services provider. The retailer may target certain customers for additional financial service products, working with the financial services provider to identify which customers are the best prospects.

TOP VANILLA

In this approach, leadership is achieved by offering excellent customer management (before, during and after the sale), but to standards available to everyone in the target market rather than just a few selected customers. In some cases, this is combined with one of the other approaches for one or more small segments of highly valuable customers. Interestingly, some of the most successful practitioners of this – sometimes using some personalized communication – are intermediaries. In the UK, Viking Direct (office supplies) and RS Components (electronic parts) come to mind as providers of a very high standard of service to all their customers.

This 'top vanilla' approach is characteristic of companies that manage their customers entirely by direct marketing techniques such as telemarketing, direct mail and the Internet. However, it must not be confused with disintermediated approaches as many of the most successful users of this approach are intermediaries. The reason for this is that their objective is to push as much third-party product through their 'sales engine' as possible. Their strength lies in the simplicity of the business model, which is shown in simplified form in Figure 2.1.

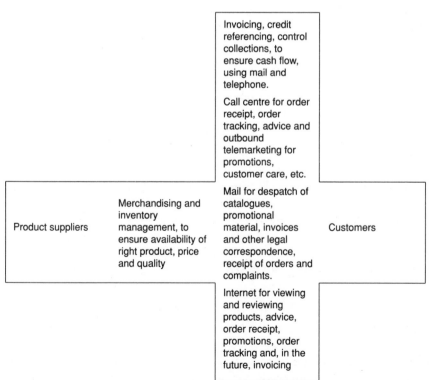

Figure 2.1 *The simple direct intermediary model*

SPOT-SELL WITHIN A MANAGED ROSTER

Some customers, for some or all of the products they buy, prefer to get the best deal (value for money, not necessarily lowest price) at the time of purchase, but only from a selected roster of suppliers. This is characteristic of heavy users of FMCG or shopping goods, but also of many industrial purchases, where a roster of suppliers is used to ensure optimal variety, product quality and service. In such situations, attempts to develop behavioural loyalty (so that a customer buys more than his or her normal proportion from one supplier) usually require some promotional incentive.

Branding is usually a critical determinant of inclusion in the roster and of the share of the customer's business obtained by each company within the roster. Also, for products bought via intermediaries, the supplier's aim is to ensure availability via intermediaries in the customer's roster. Note that the final customer may have a roster of products/brands and a roster of intermediaries. This situation is quite common in retail travel booking, where a customer will contact a limited number of agents, asking about the products of a limited number of companies, or having an informal company roster that is used to reject certain suggestions made by the agent.

So, in this model, marketing focuses on getting on the customer's roster and providing best value when compared to other companies on it. Top vanilla service can add competitive edge. CRM can be used to reinforce the suppliers' or intermediaries' position in the roster, though it may not help in gaining 'share of wallet'. However, if a supplier's product or the intermediary's offer is good value for money, they will obtain a 'fair share' of the business, so the returns for CRM can be good.

SPOT-SELL MANAGED BY AN AGENT

In some cases, drawing up the roster can be a complicated task, with which customers feel they need the help of an agent – whether for expert advice, bargaining expertise or even just to delegate some of the transaction management. Also, some modes of purchase may require them to sign on as a registered customer (such as when buying by telephone or on the Web), but they prefer to register with an independent agent rather than with the original supplier of the product or service. So, the customers appoint an intermediary to act as an agent and the agent then draws up the roster. Examples of this kind of behaviour include financial services and travel. In this situation, agent marketing becomes the key to success, the final customers having less influence on the purchase as choice has been delegated. However, CRM techniques can be used very successfully with the intermediaries. This is because they will tend to include suppliers in the roster, if they, for example:

▓ recognize the amount of business the intermediary gives them by additional concessions, some of which may be passed on to the final customers;
▓ make it easy for the intermediary to do business with them – it is amazing how many companies do not treat intermediaries as customers, preferring instead to focus on the final customer;
▓ facilitate the tasks that have to be completed by the intermediary and final customer together;
▓ bring more customers to the intermediary.

This approach can often be combined with top vanilla service for final customers and agents. In an increasing number of cases, the agent may be Web-based. In its most extreme case, auctioning of airline seats or hotel rooms is undertaken by Web agents, with customers specifying price limits. This may be combined with a roster limitation.

An alternative to this slightly adversarial idea of agents spot-buying on behalf of customers is the idea of partnership customer management.

PURE SPOT-SELL

Here, the customer rejects all relationships and buys – whether from an original supplier or intermediary – purely on the basis of current perceived value. This, in turn, is strongly influenced by classic marketing mix variables – brand, perceived product quality, price (including promotional discounts), availability and so on. Good examples of this are purchases made in the newly deregulated energy market, the direct banking short-term savings market and Web-based auctions (although if you have a favourite auction Web site you might be considered to have appointed an agent). In these cases, perhaps surprisingly, classic marketing mix variables become more important – particularly brand image and customer service. To avoid being drawn into this situation, suppliers must seek to differentiate their offer such that the customer sees pure spot-buying as being risky.

CHANNEL PARTNERSHIP

This is a model that seems to have a very good pedigree, but is quite difficult to implement. It is suggested as a model in those instances where both supplier and intermediary have strong visibility of and to the final customer, as in the automotive industry or in financial services. It is the model we are most often asked about, so we need to spend some time explaining it and its requirements for success.

The general ideas behind the model are as follows.

- If both supplier and intermediary (the 'partners') use CRM techniques on the final customer, then both will gain.
- For them to work together in this way, a true partnership approach is needed.
- This approach normally also requires business-to-business CRM techniques to be used between the supplier and intermediary. For example, intermediaries are managed according to their current and potential future value, their propensity to work in partnership, exchange data and so on.
- Partners need to accept that customers will decide which relationships, if any, they want to have with which partners, and it is up to the partners to decide which relationships they would like to have and how to motivate customers to take them up. Customers do not classify themselves as 'owned'. Also, in many cases, customers decide which needs they want to meet by which means, based on the value they perceive each of these means delivers.
- If this approach is taken, it cannot work tactically, as this will lead to conflicts caused by the fact that differences in objectives and requirements are supposed to have been sorted out. It

needs to work strategically. For example, if the intermediary or supplier decides that they wish to make increased use of CRM techniques with final customers, then the results for both will be better if they plan to work together on this from the beginning.

■ If supplier and intermediary are not working in partnership, both sides need to determine potential partnership objectives – deepening the relationship with the existing final customer base or broadening the customer base, for example.

■ Whether for existing or potential future partnerships, rules and rights in managing the relationship must be determined, as should the way in which the policy processes of each partner should correspond.

■ The key to success is trust between organizations involved, and that is easier said than done!

■ The overall success of a partnered CRM programme will be in the hands of final customers, and they will choose to access and compare an organization's propositions by different means if they have access to them. They will measure the organization using all of these!

CLASSIC MARKETING MODELS

There are several classic marketing models where the nature of customer management is not specified explicitly, but where there is a very strong implicit model of customer management. These include:

■ retailing;
■ salesforce management – especially in business-to-business marketing, which is where the oldest model of relationship marketing was born, based on ideas of key account management, industrial buying centres, quality and customer service;
■ mail order – the source of the earliest and, in some ways, still the most professional ideas of mass relationship marketing, such as customer value, customer retention and dismissal;
■ consumer product and company brand management;
■ business product management – closely related to technical innovation models.

MAKING SENSE OF THIS

Obviously, these paradigms overlap and suppliers may find that they need to combine them in different ways to manage different customers and for different products. However, each has characteristic and very different patterns of marketing investment and return.

The choice is affected by factors such as the following:

- state and rate of change of product technology – this can lead customers to require uncertainty reduction (available within the relationship or from agents), but it can also create big differences in spot value;
- underlying production and distribution techniques and costs, such as costs associated with variety, economies of scale and so on;
- rate of entry of 'new to category' customers, which affects the role of experience;
- market structure fundamentals, such as patterns of competition or regulation;
- transfer of learning and expectations customers bring to different paradigms of customer management that they experience;
- customer behaviour and psychographics (or, in simpler terms, what they think and feel, how they buy, their need to give or take control and associated lifestyle and lifecycle issues);
- timing issues – how quickly customers' needs can be identified and responded to;
- customer expertise – whether or not customers are good at identifying their own needs and, if so, how long it takes – and associated learning issues;
- sector – there is a strong tendency in some complicated business-to-business relationships for customers to prefer CRM-managed repertoires with spot-buying;
- state of intermediation – the type of intermediation (by agents, Web-based or otherwise) and amount and type of value added by intermediaries;
- relationship between risk and value – for example, whether or not customers have high risks (credit, insurance, say) attached to them as individuals and what the balance is between good

and bad customers and between good and bad customer characteristics;

■ data issues – quality, legal issues;
■ staffing – current skill levels, possibilities of recruiting new skill sets, training options and so on;
■ systems culture of the supplier – for example, whether or not the managers are able to cope with the latest call centre and Web-based technology.

THE PARADOX OF TECHNOLOGICAL PROGRESS

Many writers on relationship marketing have argued that improved ability to capture, manage and use customer information and interact with customers implies that managing customer relationships over many transactions (an element of CRM and one-to-one relationships) becomes a more appropriate strategy than previous ones. However, there is much evidence that this technological progress also makes transparent marketing and spot-buying easier, in ways that may reduce customer loyalty. Here are some of the examples and themes that we have identified.

Utilities – buying energy under the new supply arrangements

In newly deregulated markets, such as in the UK, the model for electricity or gas supply is that the individual has a relationship with the supply company. The customer signs on and agrees to buy power from that company. The company proceeds to buy electricity via the best route. This can lead to a CRM model (cross-selling of different power sources and associated household and financial services) or personalized standard marketing. However, IBM has shown simulations of a Web-based agent, which offers the customer a choice of energy sources, such as green, fossil or of a particular geographical origin. In this situation, customers can log on and switch the source of their power according to price fluctuations and so on. A consumer might, for example, be green at heart, but set an upper price limit to greenness, switching to fossil fuel if green electricity becomes too expensive. This would be agent-managed spot-selling, with the agent possibly being Web-based. In its extreme form, of course, the consumer would set the computer to do the task, defining control parameters so that the source could be switched without human intervention.

Buying a telephone call

Gone are the days when a customer had access to only one form of telephony. Today, a higher-value family might have four or five telephony providers – PTT (such as BT), cable, a low-cost supplier (usually requiring an access code to route the call off the local PTT or cable route), and one or more mobile providers, for example. In theory, customers could make calls, choosing the supplier with the best rate for each one. Indeed, this can actually be done automatically using software. Further, as multipurpose handsets become common, consumers may come to expect this. This is roster spot-buying. Customers' attempts to do this may be slowed down by the price confusion strategies employed by incumbent telephony operators. However, for specific types of call (such as to friends and family overseas, repeated and/or lengthy long-distance calls to the same number), some customers will be motivated to compare different providers and select the one that is the best value.

Under carrier pre-selection – due to arrive in Europe early in 2000 – customers will be able to buy their local telephony services in precisely the same way as they do utilities, irrespective of who owns the local loop. This development is due to EU competition law. We can expect the entry of a variety of consumer brands, in the same way that they have entered the market for Internet provision. In this case, the market may move away from spot-buying and towards the utility situation, with contractual spot-buying from a roster (annual or even shorter period contracts with a number of suppliers). However, this may also lead to the selection of several suppliers according to relative rates for different destinations or types of call (data, video or voice).

Credit v. pre-paid mobiles

The enormous take-up of pre-paid mobiles (in Italy these account for over 50 per cent of the stock) indicates that many customers are happy with the classic product/brand model, with no relationship. Some customers may be influenced to buy their top-ups from particular stores by CRM techniques (such as double points on a store loyalty card – and the margin is there to allow this). Highest value customers may accept a CRM approach with the network provider if their company is paying the bill and they get a free incentive, such as Air Miles. However, most users (and most new users) are not in the latter category.

Short-term savings

The invasion of retailers (Sainsbury's, Safeway, Tesco) and insurers (Standard Life Bank, Prudential Egg) using direct marketing (mainly call centre, but in one case the Web) has caused very large numbers of customers to switch their savings away from retail banks. Effectively, consumers line up one or more companies on their roster (stepped interest rates and family group interest rates make it likely that most will have only one provider at a time). They then switch money to and fro according to the amount of cash they have (or expect to have) spare. However, they have a very specific product objective in doing so. This is one of the few areas where value for money is completely transparent.

Cross-selling in financial services

Financial services markets are characterized by generally low levels of cross-buying (and suspect profitability of much cross-selling as most companies practise it). This indicates that most consumers are happy to use the variety of channel/marketing/IT options available to them (direct mail response, call centre – often stimulated by direct response TV) to choose each supplier based on perceived value for money. Also, because consumers' timing is hard to predict for lifecycle products (such as life assurance and pensions), they are hard to cross-sell to. This is why many life assurance and pensions companies – which still gain much of their business via intermediaries – are shocked when they get their first data warehouse and realize how low their cross-selling ratio is. Some companies have now developed a more targeted approach to cross-selling as a result. In some cases based on best practice, software works on the basis of products being marketed to customers according to their propensity to buy, rather than customers being selected according to the probability that they will help the product manager meet targets. However, success rates are still usually fairly low. This is because as customers become more aware of the different offers, they are more likely to follow a roster spot-buy policy and call centres and the Internet make this much easier.

Grocery food buying

This is the classic roster spot-buy. Here, there seems to be much evidence that the more a consumer buys of a particular category, the wider the roster goes and spot-buying (between brands and, to some extent, between stores) takes place within this. In fact, much retail buying is catchment area determined, but we can already see the situation developing in which retailers post their price lists and special offers on the Web, the consumer applies a standard template shopping list and works out which store offers the best deal.

Interestingly, in this world, the brand suppliers are finding ways to develop relationships with their final customers. Most have very active Web sites, designed to capture customer information and draw their customers' attention to their latest offers. However, classic direct mail approaches are also working well, such as those operated by the Unilever/Cadbury/Kimberley Clark consortium, Jigsaw.

Financial service advisers

One of the reasons for generally low cross-selling ratios – particularly in life assurance and pensions – is that the greater the value of the final customers, the more likely it is that they will see independent advisers, who will spot-recommend based on value to the customers and (taking into account commission) value to the advisers. Very few companies offer incentives to existing product holders – usually this area is not explored, nor is the second relationship known about. This is agent-managed spot-buying.

Buying a rail or air journey – including seat auctions

The Web and, of course, the call centre, videotext and global distribution systems, make it much easier for customers to find the best mode, routeing and price for a given journey. Agent-managed spot-buying is encouraged by Global Distribution Systems suppliers, such as Sabre, by their use of Web technology (www.travelocity.com). CRM techniques work for corporate customers who receive personal incentives (miles). The low-cost airlines are concentrating on providing a medium vanilla product.

Car buying

Surveys by motor companies themselves indicate that many consumers intensely dislike the process by which they are forced to enter into a relationship with a car dealer when their preference is for roster spot-buying at a retailer. Slowly, both fleet and private markets are moving in this direction, as described in our research into customer management in the automotive industry (Stone, M et al, 1998, *Managing Automotive Customers*, Policy Publications). In Europe, where legal constraints apply (the EU Block Exemption that allows motor manufacturers to force sole brands on dealers), the move is, of course, hampered. However, hypermarkets are making their plans! Carrefour in France has already moved into the motor market, and Tesco in the UK had to scotch rumours of such a move when it bought a large number of Skoda Octavias for a promotion – the advertisement read 'We're not selling cars, we're giving them away'. (For some interesting insights into the mindset of major retailers and how it influences their thinking about new product and service areas, see Mason, T, 1998, The best shopping trip? How Tesco keeps the customer satisfied, *Journal of the Market Research Society*, 40 (1), pp 5–12, and Shingleton, J, 1998, Development of petrol retailing in the United Kingdom, *Journal of the Market Research Society*, 40 (1), pp 13–23.)

THE IMPACT OF WEB-BASED MARKETING ON THESE MODELS

Formerly a concern only for those in the US, marketers all over the world are now focusing on what difference the Web makes to their marketing models. Serious analysis of the requirements for translating practices developed in the era of telephone- and mail-based database marketing is now being carried out – not just for developed economies, but also for the more hybrid situations that pertain in the Pacific Rim or Eastern Europe (see, for example, Chang, S, 1998, Cutting-edge Internet database marketing to the Pacific Rim region, *Journal of Database Marketing*, 5 (3), pp 255–66, and Howard, M and Cornish, C, 1998, How can direct marketers improve the quality of relationship marketing on the Internet?, *New Marketing Directions*, 1 (4), pp 3–11, and 1998, Setting up e-business in the Czech Republic, *E-Business – A Working Reality*, IBM Corporation). Prescriptive literature now exists on how to market via the Web (see Lewis, H G and R, 1997, *Selling on the Net: The complete guide*, NTC Business Books). Perhaps more importantly, the implications of the Web for the entire business process are now being explored and, at the same time, its likely effects on the future role of the marketing concept and all customer-facing functions (see, for example, Tapscott, D, Lowy, A and Ticoll, D (eds), 1998, *Blueprint to the Digital Economy*, McGraw-Hill, or Martin, C, 1999, *Net Future*, McGraw-Hill).

The general conclusion from all this work is that the Web has freed the consumer from the constraints of physical (that is, non-virtual) channels of communication and distribution. More informed consumers can construct their own channels from a variety of offers. They can decide to conduct some aspects of their buying direct with suppliers, in other cases via agents. They may get information from agents and buy direct or vice versa. Another conclusion is that the Web can accelerate the processing of business – and put at risk those companies that are slow to react to, or anticipate, customers' needs, new competitors or even new types of competition. At the same time, companies that use the Web as an opportunity to give customers more information can save costs and improve customer service (such as logistics companies' package-tracking services).

3

The Customers' Perspective

Two key questions face you when you are considering whether or not to adopt the idea of CRM.

- What types of CRM policy are required?
- How far should each policy go?

The answers to both these questions lie to a great extent in your customers' needs and perceptions.

CUSTOMERS' REQUIREMENTS

Customers are reasonable. Many are quite realistic about the relationship you can provide and know that you are constrained by resources, technology and the problems of managing change. Customers whose expectations are unrealistic can be educated as to what is realistic.

In analysing your customers' views about their relationship with you, you must understand that the period during which your customers consider themselves to be in a relationship with you may be quite long. Opportunities to strengthen this relationship occur throughout this period, particularly just before, during and immediately after your transactions with them.

In their relationship with you, your customers may distinguish between major contact episodes and less important ones. For example, a car being booked in for its annual service may start with a minor contact episode – calling to book the service. The next step may be more significant – telling the service manager what problems the car has got or putting these in writing. Then comes the day of the service, when the customer leaves the car at the garage. The customer may be worried all day. Uncertainty may be felt about whether or not the car will be ready on time, whether or not all faults will be rectified and what the cost will be. Then comes what is arguably the most important contact of all – when the customer collects the car and pays the bill. Close relationship management at this point is critical. If the car is going to take longer to service, the customer should be telephoned to let them know this, if possible. This will prevent the awful situation of the customer having to wait for the car, which adds to the customer's uncertainty. For example, the customer may wonder if being told that the car is being waited for will cause service staff to hurry and not do the job properly.

So, your customers' relationship requirements will usually vary according to what *they* consider to be the significance of each transaction with you and of the overall relationship. In our example of a car service, before booking in the car, the customer may want a list of service items, costs and incentives and a calendar of available dates. When booking in the car, the customer may require brisk and efficient service. When confronted with the bill, the customer may require careful explanation of why the service cost so much!

Levels of relationship

The idea of the level of relationship your customers expect must be expressed more concisely if you are to base policy on it. We define level of relationship to include:

■ the media by means of which the contacts take place – mail, telephone, face-to-face encounters and so on;
■ the frequency of contacts – timing may be an important element here;
■ who each contact is with – which part of your organization, which individual and so on;

■ the scope of each contact – what subjects are covered;
■ the information exchanged in each contact;
■ the outcomes of each contact – that is, the next steps for both the customer and yourself;
■ the cost of each contact to the customer – not just in terms of money, but in time and stress involved.

In most cases, customers have an idea about the **minimum acceptable** relationship and the **desired** level. If customers already have experience of dealing with you, there may also be a **perceived** level – the level they perceive they receive. Perceived levels contrast with *actual* levels, which are statements from your point of view as to what relationship actions were definitely carried out.

Note that *perceptions* about contacts (type, frequency and so on) often vary significantly from *actual* attributes, and are often subject to a **halo effect**. This effect has a sliding scale – the better a customer's relationship with you, the more positive his or her perception of each contact. For example, loyal customers may believe that they are in contact more frequently with you than they actually are (perhaps because you are 'front of mind' for them) and may have a more positive view of each contact than is warranted from what actually occurred.

It is equally important to not be providing too much! The best example of this is the **over-attentive** relationship – contact that is too frequent, giving or asking for too much information and so on. In telemarketing, if a customer calls the response-handling centre and the call is answered immediately after the first ring, he or she has no time to think after dialling. This 'thought collection' time is particularly important in countries that are switching from older methods of call connection to electronic methods, where the ring follows the dialling much more quickly. If, coupled with this, the telephone operator is too quick and aggressive (from the customers' perspective) with the opening dialogue, customers may feel threatened and a barrier to future calls from the customer will be formed. Older customers may find all this particularly difficult to cope with.

Some customers may have threshold levels of satisfaction and dissatisfaction. Relationship standards that fall below their threshold may be strongly criticized, but, once at the level of the threshold, that performance may be taken for granted. There may also be a band of relationship attributes within which they are more or less indifferent.

What determines the relationship your customers want?

Here are some of the factors that determine the kind of relationship customers want.

The effect of experience

Customers form requirements and perceptions as a result of several influences. The most important of these is experience, whether this is with you, a competitor or some other benchmark company. All suppliers of products and services are, in some sense, in competition with each other when it comes to CRM. In a consumerist age, it is not unusual to hear customers making explicit comparisons, say, between a retail store and a rail company.

The extent to which customers make such 'parallel' comparisons has been increased by the consumerist values of our age. As leading commercial organizations improve their CRM, so public service organizations are under pressure to do the same. This is because customers do compare and they form expectations that are transferred across different suppliers of products and services.

In a competitive environment, customers who stay in relationships with particular suppliers do so because the total package they receive from the supplier – product, service, price, credit, relationship and so forth – is right for them. However, there is no room for complacency. Customers of suppliers charging low prices may have talked themselves into accepting the idea that low relationship standards are worth tolerating because of the low price charged. However, if competition emerges that still charges low prices but has high standards of CRM, these customers' requirements may change.

Behaviour may lag behind experience. A supplier with a good relationship record may occasionally lapse. Perhaps surprisingly, its customers do not immediately switch suppliers. They have learned that their supplier has provided good experiences in the past. This learning takes time to undo. This customer behaviour gives suppliers the opportunity to recover.

Word of mouth

The power of word of mouth is often spoken of in terms of how satisfied or dissatisfied customers communicate their experiences to others. Customers who are totally satisfied – or else are dissatisfied and then have their problems resolved by you – can become powerful advocates for you. They will recommend you to their friends. If the latter are dissatisfied with their supplier, then such recommendations can be particularly effective.

The force of recommendation is as powerful in organizational markets as it is in customer markets. Information about relationships may be communicated within the buying centre – the group of staff who make or influence the buying decision – and to other buying centres. In buying centres that are making important, high-risk decisions, it is particularly important for members of the buying centre to be, and appear to be, knowledgeable. Any piece of information about the experiences of others is often seized upon and given great status.

The time problem

Despite shorter working hours and longer holidays, many customers are less tolerant of the time it takes to interact with a supplier than they used to be. Perceived scarcity of free time can make customers want to achieve more in a short time. This can also make your customers worry about the differences between what they want to achieve and what they actually achieve and, of course, what others achieve.

If your customers feel they are short of time, saving them time may be an important relationship proposition. However, the time problem varies by age group. The older and richer the customers, the less they perceive that there is a time problem. Marketers focusing on older customers, therefore, may well promote the length of time they are prepared to spend with customers. This applies particularly for more up-market products.

The buying decision

The nature of the buying decision can be classified using the 'buygrid', a concept borrowed from industrial marketing. It defines certain 'buyclasses', as follows.

■ **New task** The customer has no experience of the product or service type. In this case, the customer will need a lot of information and may ask friends or colleagues about it. You are trying to make the sale and establish a relationship at the same time – not an easy task. If you push too hard to make the sale, your later relationship with this customer may be poor, because he or she may have been sold the wrong product or service.

■ **Straight rebuy** A routine reorder without any modification, often handled routinely. If you are already supplying to a particular customer, your key CRM objective is to facilitate reordering, but also to ensure that your customer considers what else he or she can buy from you at the same time.

■ **Modified rebuy** Where the customer seeks to change supplier or some other aspect of the purchase, but wants the same general kind of product or service. Modified rebuys often provide the greatest test of the quality of CRM. Your customer is considering whether or not to switch products or services and so may switch away from you if you mismanage the relationship.

High-involvement and low-involvement decisions

Many purchases require little or no explanation. Often, the motivation to make a purchase is already understood. In other instances there is little that needs to be understood. This is particularly true of routine purchases, such as a bus trip by a customer who makes the same trip every day. Basic products and services are commodities. They are purchased for functional reasons and carry little or no symbolic meaning. Their unit price is low, whichever brand is selected. They are routinely purchased. The risk a customer takes by making the wrong choice of supplier or product is low because economic, psychological and social commitment to the product is low. These are low-involvement products. However, not all low-price, frequently purchased products or services are low-involvement products. Commuting journeys by train are certainly not!

Customers sometimes feel that there is a high psychological and social risk involved in making the wrong choice. This applies particularly when the choice is 'worn' or the experience shared with others. Many products are 'worn' – not just clothes, but also drinks, cars, books, home furnishings and the like. These are high-involvement products and services. They are particularly important for CRM. Good CRM in high-involvement situations greatly reinforces customer loyalty. Poor CRM in such situations leads to customer disloyalty and strong word of mouth condemnation.

If a decision is important to the customer, then considerable thought may be devoted to the purchase. If the product is bought frequently, more thinking is likely to take place when the customer is considering switching between suppliers or products. Once the new purchasing pattern has been established as a habit, purchases are likely to take place routinely, without much thought.

Stage of the buying cycle

Usually, customers go through a number of stages – sometimes sequentially, sometimes combining different ones.

■ **Existence of the need**   The need comes into existence. Your customer may not be aware of it, but it is there.
■ **Identification or realization of need**   The need moves to 'front of mind'.
■ **Problem recognition**   The need exists for a reason, typically because a problem needs to be solved (such as meeting a want). Your customer recognizes that the problem exists.
■ **Search for information**   Your customer seeks information about products and services to solve the problem. This is triggered by the need for a resolution.
■ **Evaluation**   All the relevant accessible information required to make the choice that will resolve the problem is gathered and analysed. Your customer may or may not have established choice criteria. Even if they have done so, during evaluation these may change. Patterns of deliberation are also important. Some customers rely more on personal advice than on information provided by suppliers. So, the outcome of the evaluation depends on various factors, varying from personality and past experience to the ways in which different suppliers provide information. You must understand the criteria your customers use to evaluate different suppliers, products and services. This is the link between CRM and financial success, for, if the relationship determines choices made between suppliers, products and services, then the commercial justification for investing in creating and managing the relationship is not difficult to find.
■ **Choice**   Some choices are impulsive or at least seem so to others. Many, though, are deliberate and rational, based on systematic processing of information. Such processing leads

first to the formation of an intention to purchase, which is determined by the formulation of beliefs about the product and its likely performance.

▓ **Post-purchase review** After the decision, your customer re-evaluates it in the light of any new information, such as that on the product's performance. In some post-purchase situations, customers experience cognitive dissonance – that is, they feel unhappy about what they now know. They may experience doubt, even anxiety, if the product did not come up to expectations. This may be resolved in various ways. They may look for information that supports their decision, such as from others who made the same decision. They may focus on the good deal they got in an attempt to convince themselves that they made the right decision. They may even ignore, avoid or distort incoming information that is inconsistent with what they want to believe. CRM after the sale can help your customers justify the decision they made, even if there are problems at that point.

BRANDING AND CUSTOMER LOYALTY

When it comes to the purchase, corporate and product/service branding are very important. However, they also have a strong effect on your customers' expectations and perceptions of their relationship with you. A strong brand, developed over a long period, gives the relationship a strong platform. Without it, the relationship almost has to start from scratch with every transaction.

Customer loyalty and branding are closely connected. Highly visible and positive branding cannot exist without customer loyalty. Equally, customer loyalty depends on the relationship, in the long run. If you manage relationships with your customers well, the customers will tend to be loyal and this will provide the opportunity for branding to get to work. Branding requires the strong imprinting of ideas about the product in customers' minds. These ideas will be positive if customers have frequent good experiences in buying and using your products or services and in communications with you.

The key manifestation of disloyalty is when a customer switches suppliers or brands. Sometimes this occurs when your customers decide they need a change, not because of any problem with what they have been buying from you or how you have managed the relationship with them, but simply as a result of a search for variety or a different specification. This cannot be avoided, although good CRM can encourage such customers to return. Switches due to big price differences are also hard to prevent by means of CRM, unless the cheaper product is of a lower quality than yours.

Switches due to problems with your product or service or poor CRM can and should be avoided. The unresolved problem that you do not know about is the most dangerous. It festers and, eventually, your customer switches away. CRM that encourages complaints and ensures that they are dealt with well is the best defence against this cause of switching.

Control

Your customers will often be motivated by a need for security. This may lead to a need to be in control of their relationship with you. However, many relationship situations create a perception among customers that they are totally without control, such as the unsolicited telesales call in the evening that the customer does not know how to terminate.

So, every attempt should be made to explore how to give customers who wish to be in control the feeling of control. The idea of locus of control is useful for analysing this situation. In many marketing situations, the locus of control is with you. You determine which marketing actions will take place and when. However, as with all marketing, it is the *perceived* locus of control that is more important than the *actual* locus of control. Customers can be persuaded to think that they are in control.

If your customers' control is less than they want or, indeed, if they feel that they are being asked to control a situation when they are incapable of doing so because they are, for example, unqualified or without the right information, levels of stress can rise. This can result in anxious and uncooperative behaviour. Research shows that the need for control does not depend on obvious factors, such as customers' purchasing power. It is a complicated mixture of elements that are as much to do with the customers' individual personality as they are with any other factor. So, you need to give customers the degree of control they want – that is, give real control – or take over control yourself. If a new product requires, for its success, for customers to be in control (because of a high self-service element, for example), then customer education must be a key part of the product launch package. The nature of the education package will, of course, vary with the ability of target customers to absorb such instructions.

Some customers prefer to be in complete control. However, a customer who prefers self-service for a routine sales transaction may prefer your close attention for a more complicated one. Other customers do not want to be in control. Their need for security may be best fulfilled by cocooning them, so that they do not have to take any initiative. Wherever possible, you should offer the two main options – control or to be managed.

AUTOMATION

CRM can be delivered via a variety of media, depending on the nature of the contact. Information can be provided face to face, on the telephone, via the Internet or other electronic media, on a video screen, on a TV by means of video on demand, via a loudspeaker or in print. Replacement of people-based marketing by automated CRM provides a challenge to relationship delivery. The best examples of this are in simple transactions. These include:

▪ Web-based transactions;
▪ telephone directory enquiries or provision of other information via an automated helpline;
▪ self-service petrol and car wash;
▪ video hire via a machine.

These transactions are handled best if you examine the full range of customers' needs that are to be satisfied by the automated approach. Often, while carrying out a simple transaction, customers take the opportunity to check facts or receive information. When withdrawing or crediting money, a customer may seek information about account balances or clearing of recent transactions. Those renting videos might seek information about the popularity of certain titles. Sometimes, such information can be provided automatically as part of the transaction.

FOLLOWING THE SCRIPT

In many relationship situations, your staff are trained to follow a script. Customers can also be trained or educated to expect a script and then follow it. If customers agree to follow the script, the chances of the transaction and relationship being successful increase because the script is designed to identify their needs and then guide them through the process of receiving the right response from you. This is at its most explicit in a telemarketing script. If your customers can be conditioned to expect questions to identify their needs and then cooperate in subsequent actions to ensure that the contact succeeds, then both your and your customers' objectives will be achieved.

Customers who prefer to be in control must be handled more carefully, and systems and scripts designed and staff trained so that these customers believe it is they who are scripting the situation, even though you are in control of the logic and the coverage of the script. For customers who want control, this may be the single most important part of the relationship mix.

Customers still have a tendency to ignore the script. Perhaps the best example of this is failure to read instructions – the part of the script that precedes human intervention. This may be because this early part of the script is badly written or presented. It is more likely that once customers need to be in contact, they prefer human media to printed media.

Some companies use expert computer systems to help manage the dialogue with different kinds of customers and in different service situations. Obviously, this is easiest in telephone contact situations, but the approach is also used to provide instant simulations of the outcomes of different financial arrangements (life assurance, pensions) or the costs and benefits of different major computer configurations.

ORGANIZING CUSTOMER ANALYSIS

This chapter has shown the variety of attitudes that your customers may have in relation to CRM and how these attitudes are affected by the nature of the buying process. In Chapter 4, our focus switches to you – the supplier.

4

The Company's Perspective

THE NEED FOR A SECOND LOOK

Up to this point, CRM issues have been viewed through your customers' eyes. This chapter sees them through your eyes.

Most managers would agree that, in the long run, a close relationship with customers is important to success. In the short run, however, your organizational structures, control processes, procedures and operational necessities often bring you and your customers into conflict. The secret of competitive CRM does not, therefore, lie in programmes that only deal with the immediate interface between your customers and you. CRM, which usually works in terms of both the short and long run, requires you to reconsider every aspect of policy.

PLANNING FOR CRM

Your ability to meet customers' relationship needs depends on:

■ **your objectives**   what you aim to achieve and whether or not these objectives require customer relationships to be managed;
■ **your strategies**   the translation of objectives into the main lines of policy;

■ **your policies and action plans** the translation of strategies into practical work;
■ **your processes and procedures** the norms and rules by which your staff work;
■ **your resources** which are allocated to achieving different policies;
■ **your people** who can contribute so much to CRM – if they are wrongly allocated, managed or trained, their effect on customer relationships can be devastating;
■ **your planning processes** which match your resources to objectives and harness resources via particular policies, working to particular procedures;
■ **your systems** the right data, available to the right people, at the right time will enable your management process to happen;
■ **your ability to monitor key performance indicators.**

The effect of each of the above on CRM depends on whether or not your focus on customer needs is maintained. This, in turn, depends on how you use customer information.

The role of customer information

Information about your customers and their needs should be taken into account during the planning process and be available in a usable form at specified points of contact with the customer. These points of contact may be inbound (the customer contacts you) or outbound (you contact the customer) across a variety of contact types (orders, complaints, general enquiries, sales enquiries, billing queries, technical queries and so on). Using data in this way, for both planning and communication purposes, is important in 'delivering the strategy' and making your plans more visible to your customers.

Systems, procedures, scripts and boundaries

The idea of the 'script' governing the relationship between you and your customers is an essential part of CRM. What you see as a set of procedures should be thought of as a customer script (not necessarily something to control the flow of one conversation, but something to control the overall dialogue), for situations in which the customer is interacting with you. If the script is followed, there is a reasonable assurance that the quality of the outcome of the transaction or relationship will be as required. The script therefore needs to be worked out carefully, communicated to your customers and, where necessary, form the basis of customer training (for complicated scripts).

The script is also a way of giving your customers a perceived level of control. If your customers learn the script properly, the contact episode can be effectively managed by them. A good script can make your customer feel that the outcome of the episode is more predictable, too, reducing stress levels. For example, if the script begins with them providing their customer number, all the data can be on-hand. Of course, not all your customers require a high degree of control, so a script may not be necessary if each service episode is managed with close personal attention.

Learning from experience

Knowledge is the key to CRM and is of two kinds:

- ▨ **knowledge of your customers** what they currently perceive, need and expect and how this situation may change in the future;
- ▨ **knowledge of your own organization** its capabilities, what it actually delivers to your customers and how both of these will be affected by future policies.

Knowledge of customers

Knowledge of customers can be gained in many ways. These include:

- ▨ formal market research and observation;
- ▨ transaction information – responses and enquiries, sales and so on;
- ▨ competitive information – what your customers are buying from other suppliers;
- ▨ complaints and compliments;
- ▨ feedback from your customer-facing staff.

The key issue here is whether or not your organization is sufficiently customer-oriented – does it demand and thrive on feedback from customers or does it regard customer information as an intrusion into its work? CRM cannot succeed without a thirst for customer feedback and a proper process for collecting this feedback, digesting it and identifying from it any opportunities for improving CRM.

Knowledge of your own organization

The two key questions that need to be answered here are the following.

■ How is your organization structured to deliver CRM?
■ How is your organization managed to deliver CRM?

In a large organization, with many tiers of management, or with many branches or subsidiaries, these questions must be asked at each level.

Structuring to deliver CRM is a question of putting the authority to give individual customers what they want as close to your customers as possible, while concentrating responsibility for relationship management in that part of your organization that has the resources to invest in achieving it and the information flows to monitor and measure its achievement.

'Closeness' does not necessarily imply geographical proximity. Many national suppliers have found that, for handling individual relationships, central telemarketing facilities are more cost-effective than having many offices around the country that deal with customers just part-time.

Many suppliers – large and small – have also found that a key element of CRM is making it easy for customers to contact them. Until customers can do so, it is almost impossible to judge what relationship is being delivered. This is because customers may be largely cut off from the organization, except when the latter wants to contact them.

Managing the delivery of CRM is a question of having systems, management procedures and control processes in place that allow staff to meet customers' needs and recruiting, training and keeping staff informed so that they have the skills and abilities to meet these needs (this is the focus of the last part of this book).

Warning signs of CRM failures include those given in the checklist in Figure 4.1. Tick one or more of these and you will know which area you need to work on.

Are any of these warning signs apparent in your situation?	
■ Needing to refer too many individual relationship management decisions to senior managers. ■ Long lead times for YES/NO decisions. ■ Systems not allowing staff the flexibility to deal with customers' needs. ■ Work pressures not allowing staff to complete tasks (customers often go to the end of the queue in such circumstances). ■ Poor-quality information being given to staff, so that they do not know what to tell your customers. ■ Motivation, appraisal and other people-management systems giving inadequate attention to success in dealing with customers. ■ Complaint rates rising. ■ Motivation of front-line staff low. ■ Customer loss rates increasing.	

Figure 4.1 *Checklist for warning signs of poor customer management*

Learning in practice – the role of leadership

It is one thing to have lots of data and ideas about how to manage customer relationships; it is another to do something about it. This is where CRM leadership comes in. Ideally, in every organization that depends on dealing successfully with customers, all staff should be CRM-oriented. However, achieving such a situation is not easy. Change normally requires leadership. In a large organization, this leadership is required at every level. Leaders function as coach, communicator and monitor. They identify problems, propose solutions and motivate people to change. They initiate programmes to implement changes to systems and procedures. Without a good sprinkling of CRM champions around the organization, even the best CRM policies are likely to fail.

The CRM leader

The first role of the CRM leader is to make sure that the learning is properly absorbed by the organization. This means taking the conclusions to the right people and showing the evidence that CRM pays (or satisfies some other basic objective). This may mean demonstrating the severity of the problem or the competitive opportunity that has been presented.

At this stage, things can go badly wrong. Once an organization, however large or small, has accepted the need to make improvements by implementing CRM, the next step is definitely not a CRM programme. The next step is to take the idea and benefits of CRM into the core policy-making process and ensure it does its work there. Once the idea and methods of CRM have been absorbed into this process, then CRM leadership works within the procedures and systems of every department, not as a challenge to them.

The importance of a clear corporate strategy

It is easy for an organization to become confused about CRM. The 'headless chicken' analogy – running around in every direction without a clear goal – is very apt. Today, CRM consultants are two a penny. Articles extolling the virtues of CRM are part of the daily diet of managers. In this situation, a manager might rush into an ill-considered CRM programme. This would be exactly the wrong thing to do.

CRM is one approach to looking at how your organization works. Whether or not the CRM perspective is the correct one in your situation depends on what your objectives are, how you aim to achieve them and with which customers. You can only determine whether or not you should be investing more time and money in CRM by undertaking a proper analysis, which is part of your normal planning process. However, a clear corporate strategy that will pay more than simply lip-service to customer CRM is unlikely unless influential members of senior management are committed to the concept.

Gaining commitment to CRM

Before we move on to describe the essential elements of *planning* CRM, it should be said that there are several requirements you must fulfil to be able to deliver CRM. There is little chance of sustaining delivery of CRM if only one or a few of these requirements are met. For this reason, it is very important for your whole organization – however large or small – to be committed to managing relationships with customers.

In a small organization – even a sole trader business – there is less chance for great variations in attitude between members of staff. If the owner or manager is not committed to managing relationships with customers, this attitude will transfer quickly to other staff. There will be a close connection between staff behaviour and success and to the owner's or manager's criteria.

In a large company, staff working with customers can maintain standards of CRM that are not underwritten by the formal policies of their organization. The more remote these staff are from the centre of power, and the more freedom they are allowed, the longer such behaviour can continue. Eventually, however, resource pressures are likely to constrain this behaviour. Equally, staff in contact with customers may be totally unconcerned about customers.

In such situations, the lead from top management is crucial. Without it, all down the line, managers will be faced with other priorities. These include things such as short-term cost control or immediate sales achievement, avoidance of risk by sticking to procedures and the like. Staff working close to customers need strong and frequent reinforcement if they are to stick to the principles of CRM.

Strategic focus is essential to the success of CRM. However, strategic focus by itself is not enough. Your top management must also be committed to the role of CRM in achieving the desired focus and contributing to competitive positioning. If CRM is considered as insignificant relative to return on assets, and as making only a marginal contribution to it, then there is little hope for its survival. This message will be clearly transmitted down the line!

Too much has been written and spoken about 'top management commitment' for any line manager to suspend their suspicion instantly when they hear or see this phrase. It is a hackneyed phrase and therefore a warning sign. Commitment means commitment in terms of resources and seeing policies through, particularly in adversity. It is easy to subscribe to slogans; it is more difficult to implement policies that require fundamental changes of attitude. It takes time as well as money. Therefore, when the phrase 'top management commitment' is used here, it means considered commitment by top management. For this commitment to be true rather than hollow, top managers must have full knowledge of the time and resources that will be absorbed, and the problems that will be encountered along the way – particularly those relating to staff attitudes and skills.

This implies that genuine commitment must be preceded by clear communication of the costs – financial and otherwise – as well as the benefits of CRM. Where the situation allows, it should also be based on hard evidence as to the benefits, such as the results of pilot studies.

Basing commitment on understanding

It is not sensible to ask your top management to be committed to CRM unless they understand:

▓ your organization's current relationship with customers;
▓ how it can be improved;
▓ the costs and benefits of improving it.

It therefore makes sense to involve your senior management in some of the activities that usually form the 'front end' of a commitment to CRM. It is not realistic to expect commitment other than on the basis of understanding. You should involve your senior management in research into the attitudes of customers and staff, not just give a presentation of results. Ways to involve top management are given in Figure 4.2.

Continuity of commitment

The idea that commitment must be sustained has already been mentioned. However, sustaining commitment to ideas that seem very attractive is a problem. New ideas come along and replace

Which activities will appeal to your senior management?	
▓ Attendance at discussion groups. ▓ Visits (to own and competitors' five sites). ▓ Exposing them to the relationship provided by your company and your competitors. ▓ Involvement in research design and interpretation. ▓ Exposure to examples of successful and unsuccessful CRM programmes. The latter are important, as they indicate that such programmes are not easy to develop and run. Exposure should include performance indicators and financial results.	

Figure 4.2 *Checklist of ways in which to involve senior management*

them. You should always treat claims for the universal applicability of a concept with suspicion – demand hard evidence and insist on piloting. This is a solid foundation – the only foundation, in fact – for CRM. Once such a foundation has been built, it provides the basis for an enduring commitment.

Depth of commitment

Finally, the commitment must be deep – in the sense that it leads to the concept of CRM permeating all plans and delivery of those plans. This, of course, requires transfer of the commitment to those building the plans and implementing them.

Such transfer raises few problems when the drive for top management commitment has come from 'the troops' – in this case, middle managers. However, it does raise problems when it results from a top manager's own conviction, a private 'journey to Damascus', perhaps stimulated by consultants. In such cases, a programme of communication and education may be required. In particular, the 'seasoned operators' who form the core of the delivery apparatus may feel that they have 'seen it all before' – as indeed they have. These operators – salespeople, counter staff and so on – will have been subjected to many campaigns over the years. The situation will be worse if these campaigns were short-lived, producing no real benefit to the operators, disappearing like a Will O' The Wisp as soon as the environment changed.

To avoid this, CRM programmes must provide benefits – immediate and longer-term ones. This must be so not only for staff responsible for implementing them with customers, but all staff in the line of command concerned. The steady transmission of the philosophy and practices of CRM down the line is a much better solution than a quick blast of publicity with no follow-through. This implies that you must pace your approach to CRM. The approach must be durable, with steady annual improvements in the relationship and in resulting profitability.

Commitment without strain!

It is not realistic to expect senior managers to live, eat and breathe CRM all the time – they have many other responsibilities. Their role in developing and supporting CRM must therefore be closely defined. A checklist for the role of senior management is given in Figure 4.3.

As a senior manager, do you...?	
▓ Provide overall direction and guidance. ▓ Set CRM objectives and define quality standards. ▓ Support these standards by meeting regularly with staff to discuss problems and opportunities in relation to them. ▓ Create a style of teamwork that encourages staff to take responsibility for CRM and work together to improve it. ▓ Act as a role model (particularly in terms of visits to company locations). ▓ Accept responsibility for the quality of CRM. ▓ Help evaluate staff ideas on how to improve CRM. ▓ Help create a culture of orderly routine, within which your CRM objectives can be met more easily. ▓ Ensure that time is spent with new employees to introduce them to your culture and support them in their attempts to build and sustain customer relationships.	

Figure 4.3 *Checklist for the role of senior management*

More than this should not be required. However, for some companies, this role would be a radical departure from the norm. In service industries, the culture of CRM is often readily accepted, but in industries that survive by selling physical products, particularly where contact with customers is infrequent, much of the focus of senior management is on current sales levels and the performance of sales staff and so CRM often takes a back seat, to the customer's misfortune. If senior management in these industries is to take on the kinds of responsibilities listed above, it is all the more important for them to go through the kind of exposure to CRM outlined so far.

Performance indicators

If commitment to CRM is not translated into the way staff are measured or managed, then little will change. If your managers and staff hear messages about commitment, but see no change in the way that their performance is judged, they will be deeply suspicious of these messages. Some early move to change performance indicators in the direction indicated by the CRM concept is therefore recommended.

The acid test of these indicators, from top management's point of view, is how top management reacts when CRM performance indicators clash with others – financial, for example. Of course, if your company is profit-oriented and profits suddenly go deeply into the red, there is every excuse for focusing on indicators that relate to short-term profitability. Unless you survive, you will not be in the position to have any relationships with customers tomorrow. Despite this, however, there are different ways of reacting to a crisis.

Integrating performance indicators

Your top management has a particularly important role when it comes to integrating financial, technical and CRM indicators. One of the problems that many suppliers face is split responsibilities for achieving the following tasks:

- delivering quality according to specifications – that is, technical performance;
- delivering financial performance – for example, profits or satisfying a budget constraint;
- achieving relationships with customers that satisfy them.

For example, in a large industrial equipment company:

- financial staff may be responsible for pricing, setting credit terms and chasing debtors, whether for equipment sales or after-sales service;
- engineers may be responsible for performance of installed equipment;
- marketing and sales staff may be responsible for finding new customers and getting more business out of existing customers.

Each group has potentially a strong influence on CRM, but can end up pulling in opposite directions. Financial staff may alienate customers by chasing debtors. Service engineers may create dissatisfaction by questioning customers' choice of equipment ('Who sold you this, then?'). Sales staff may respond to inventory shortages by selling equipment not suitable for the customers' use, raising service costs and creating customer dissatisfaction.

The lines of control through which these different staff are managed may only merge near the top of the organization. Top management must insist that the performance of these staff is assessed partly on the basis of their help in achieving overall customer satisfaction, by virtue of their own actions or impacts on the actions of their colleagues in other departments. For example, attitude surveys should be used to provide information enabling the organization to correlate treatment of debtors with later sales levels.

Resource allocation

A final test of top management commitment is whether or not it is translated into resources. Throughout this book, the view is that, in the end, CRM pays for itself. However, in the short term, an investment may be required before a return is achieved. This investment may be in the form of training, systems or even refunds to customers. Of course, it is only fair to top management not to demand allocation of resources without evidence of benefits, but once evidence has been accepted, then the commitment should stay.

Quantifying the impact is the next key task.

5

Quantifying the Impact

ACCOUNTABILITY IN MARKETING

The adoption of CRM has many long-term effects on your business. For example, measurability of results can make your marketing function fully accountable for all its expenditure. Business results can be traced back to activities and benefits set against costs. Measurability also makes it easier to test the effectiveness of different approaches, giving the marketing function the tools needed to improve results.

However, accountability creates pressures within marketing. In many companies, the marketing function is not truly accountable for all its policies. It may be accountable in a general sense, but the information may simply not be available to hold marketing accountable for particular policies. For example, the results of a change in promotional policy or in salesforce compensation may not be accurately measurable. CRM changes this.

The question 'How much is CRM worth?' is shorthand for three further questions.

■ How much is a properly marketed-to customer worth?
■ How much difference does good CRM make?
■ What are the strategic versus tactical applications of CRM techniques?

HOW MUCH IS A PROPERLY MARKETED-TO CUSTOMER WORTH?

'Lifetime value of the customer' is not a new concept. Its pedigree comes from direct marketing (especially mail order), where long-term customer behaviour is the key to success and calculating the difference between the costs of acquiring customers and the benefits and costs of retention is the norm. The concept is also widely used in consumer goods brand management, where the key calculation is how much to spend to prevent consumers from switching brands.

In practice, managing lifetime value is a bridge too far for most companies. Very few companies have reliable estimates of the value they will derive next year from their current customers. For this reason, we prefer to use the idea of long-term value.

Calculating the value of a customer is relatively simple – the key is data. The required process is as follows:

■ determine who your target customers are;
■ identify the costs of gaining and maintaining customers and selling additional products and services to them;
■ identify the profit contribution arising from the sales made;
■ subtract one from the other to produce a stream of net contributions over the years;
■ use discounted cash flow techniques to find customers' net present value.

Using historical data about customers you already have, long-term value can be calculated and then extrapolated, making adjustments where necessary. Some companies are very uncomfortable about using past data as a predictor of future purchasing behaviour. However, in many markets it has proved the most reliable method of forecasting. An example of a long-term value calculation is given below. The steps that need to be taken are as follows.

1. Choose a segment of customers (c. 1000) fitting a defined set of criteria and recruited (gained) at the same time. The time period is not critical. If your records only go back two years, then so be it. Ideally, though, pick a five-year period.

2. Extract the revenues that have been generated by those 1000 customers each year (by campaign, season or period if you can, but it is usually not critical).
3. Calculate or estimate the annual marketing and sales cost of managing those customers. Usually a campaign cost and an apportioned cost of (field) selling will be sufficient to start with if historical records are not accurate on a per customer basis (the norm).
4. Calculate the contribution per year.
5. Apply a discounted cash flow percentage (normally available from finance departments for the calculation of financial returns on large projects) to calculate the long-term value (LTV) each year for the 1000 customers (net present value).
6. Divide the total by the number of customers to find out a 'per customer' value.
7. Model the figures, assuming you did things differently, to look at the sensitivity of the LTV. This may involve an extra campaign per year, an increase in retention rate of 2 per cent, a reduction in the cost of selling or an extra product sold into 25 per cent of the base, for example. This 'What if... ?' type analysis will indicate where the biggest effect is to be found.

The figures you end up with can then be used to determine how much to spend on CRM for each group of customers.

What does 'properly marketed to' mean?

'Properly marketed to' means that you have:

■ identified the customers' needs;
■ developed appropriate products and services to meet those needs – 'appropriate' in the sense that they are consistent with your business strategy and profit objectives;
■ marketed them to the product, with appropriate prices, channels of distribution, presentation and marketing communications.

Good marketing and customer CRM are not the same thing. For example, if you sell the wrong type of product to customers or try to manage them using the wrong distribution channel, you'll be less likely to satisfy them – however much you invest in CRM. In such circumstances, if they have a choice, they are unlikely to come back to you.

Your marketing plan, phrased in terms of its impact on your customers, should tell you the minimum customer LTV you are trying to create. However, if your marketing has not been properly focused on customers or if your CRM is weak, your marketing plan will only represent a minimum LTV. So your marketing plan should be revised when you have been through the entire CRM calculation.

HOW MUCH DIFFERENCE DOES GOOD CRM MAKE?

The answer to this depends on precisely how you do your CRM and on how your customers react to your CRM initiatives. There are no absolutes here – every company is different and every group of customers is different. The effect of good CRM can only be identified by research. This research will typically identify the following.

▓ **What kinds of contact customers perceive they have with your company**
This is called the **contact audit**. Its results often surprise managers, because they discover that their customers are in contact, or attempted contact, with their company far more often and in a greater variety of ways than they believed possible. Further, customers may often think about making contact, but be dissuaded by the difficulty of achieving it!

▓ **What the outcomes of these contacts are, in terms of the relationship**
Research is likely to produce a complicated picture here. In simple terms, a positive outcome leads to an improved CRM, but 'positive outcome' can relate to many policy areas, such as use of the right contact media, the right frequency and quality of contact, use of customer information to provide the right solution, 'right first time' solution of problems, as well as handling complaints well – a negative outcome followed by a positive outcome.

■ **How customers react to these outcomes**

Once again, the picture is likely to be far from simple. For example, well-handled complaints or time taken to adjust a product to a customer's needs may reinforce purchasing behaviour more than no-problem contacts or products that are absolutely right for the customer from the beginning. This is usually because when your customers complain, they receive higher-quality attention than is normal. Worse, it may be because the only time they receive your attention is when they complain! Also, you should be interested not only in customers who are directly affected, but also those who are told by your customers about how well you handle them. Satisfaction leads to recommendation to others, but satisfaction after good problem-resolution may lead to stronger recommendations than routinely good service! The key here is to estimate changes in long-term buying behaviour – of the customer affected and of those they tell about it. Naturally, estimates are more accurate the longer your company has been measuring the connection between good CRM and buying and recommending behaviour. However, the key need here is not for 100 per cent accuracy, but for a broad understanding of the longer-term profit implications of successful relationships.

■ **What the financial consequences are**

This is the translation of customers' relationship-affected buying behaviour into profit, as per the methodology described above.

TACTICAL VERSUS STRATEGIC APPLICATION OF CRM

Some of the techniques of CRM may be used just as tactical weapons. However, you can use CRM more effectively by taking a strategic approach and transforming how you do business. The main strategic factors that must be considered in payback calculations are:

■ competitive superiority;
■ provision of alternative sales channels;
■ setting up barriers to competitive market entry;

■ ability to develop new products and services and get them to market faster.

If you are using CRM for any of these, it means your justification for CRM is strategic. The impact cannot therefore be quantified on a 'campaign by campaign' basis.

Competitive superiority

You can establish competitive superiority by building and exploiting a database with comprehensive coverage of your existing and potential customers for your current and future products and services. You might use this capability aggressively, to win customers from your competition (conquest sales) by, for example, regular mailings to your competitors' customers. Such mailings can ask for information about customers' needs. This information can then be used to design products and marketing programmes.

Competitive superiority can also be established by means of lower costs. In many industries, the field salesperson can only make between two and five calls per day (although, in some industries, the norm may be ten). A telemarketer can make between 20 and 50 decision-maker contacts per day. The optimum competitive policy is to use field sales and telemarketing according to their relative strengths, using a customer database to coordinate the two.

Thus, the salesforce can be used where face-to-face calls are needed. This is likely to be where:

■ personal service is considered essential;
■ an important new contact is being made;
■ a difficult and sensitive problem needs to be solved;
■ a complicated presentation needs to be made;
■ in-depth diagnostic work needs to be carried out;
■ the customer asks for a sales visit;
■ on-site research is required.

A telemarketing team working off the customer database can be used for all other calls. Eventually, with appropriate teamwork between the field salesforce, telemarketing team and customers (whose time is also valuable and therefore want to be contacted by the most effective means for each call), more complicated objectives can be handled by the telemarketing team. Telemarketers may become full account managers. This approach increases the quantity and quality of contact between the salesforce and customers, without increasing the cost. It also provides greater flexibility, enabling sales effort to be redeployed more quickly to meet competitive challenges. The discipline with which sales effort is managed can be increased. For example, it can be marshalled in a more disciplined manner to mount competitive attacks on customers known to be dissatisfied with a competitive product.

Neglected customers are a problem for most businesses. In many industrial products or services markets, small business customers may be neglected. In consumer markets, neglected customers may be isolated households or those with low purchasing frequencies. For both groups, the costs of traditional sales channels may preclude contact that is frequent enough to reinforce buying behaviour. These customers may eventually switch to competitive products, assuming that your competitors have not fallen into the same trap!

CRM can help here. For example, in the small business market for certain types of office equipment (such as fax machines, photocopiers, personal computers and telephones), the direct response advertisement and the catalogue, coordinated using a customer database, is becoming the industry standard for reaching these customers. Once a prospect has become a customer, CRM can be used to maintain the dialogue, while supplies and upgrades are bought, until the equipment needs replacing, when they are likely to come to you first as a result of this contact.

CRM provides an ideal way of building loyalty and maximizing revenue. For example, the quality of customer service may be checked by a questionnaire to all customers. This could monitor customer satisfaction and intention to purchase next time. The results of the questionnaire could be used to identify problems and ensure that dissatisfied customers do not become ex-customers. Such a questionnaire could also be used to structure campaigns aimed at managing the replacement cycle. Mailings could be sent just after purchase, halfway through the expected life of the product and close to replacement decision time.

Alternative sales channels

Many businesses find that their ability to serve their customers' needs is constrained by the cost of accessing them – the cost of the sale – and are turning to CRM to solve this supply problem. If you are in this situation, CRM can lower your cost of sales by means of applications such as telemarketing, mail order, enquiry management and the like. In some industries, mail order has taken over many of the functions traditionally the preserve of sales representatives, such as is the case in the insurance industry. Customer information centres are used to reduce the costs of handling enquiries and enable sales offices to focus on the next stage of the sale. Idle enquirers and less interested customers are screened out and given other treatment, ensuring that they remain satisfied without incurring the cost of a sales call. In all these examples, the key to success is to match the cost of sales with the value of the customer.

Barriers to market entry

Businesses may find themselves unable to enter a market when faced with competitors who hold a high-quality customer database and use it effectively. In some cases, such a database can be a unique asset. The cost of setting it up may make entry difficult or impossible for other contenders. Conversely, possession of a CRM capability may be the key to entering new markets.

New products and services

Information is increasingly being regarded as a product to be sold in its own right. CRM is, by itself, creating new products and services. This new information market is in the early stages of development. Strategic alliances between database marketers are beginning to be formed. Banks, car manufacturers, financial services companies and publishers are planning new joint venture businesses, pooling the data that each possesses to build a comprehensive picture of their customers.

Quantifying CRM

In competitive strategy formulation, CRM is most frequently used to achieve one or both of the following objectives:

■ revenue defence and development;
■ cost reduction.

Many of the opportunities opened up by CRM affect both costs and revenue. Some lead to increased revenue while costs stay static or rise more slowly than revenue. Others lead to falling costs while revenue stays static or falls more slowly than costs. These effects are achieved by the development and implementation of particular applications of CRM, such as telemarketing.

Many of the changes produced have a short- and a long-term dimension. For example, telemarketing may produce cost savings and revenue increases that arise relatively quickly by reducing the cost of contacting and selling to customers and increasing market coverage. These shorter-term effects are not once and for all, but continue so long as you continue to use the application. However, the greater market coverage and reduced cost of coverage may allow you to enter different product markets. You may be able to sell a wider product range to existing customers. It may also be possible to sell information resulting from this application.

The revenue and cost changes that might result from different aspects of CRM must therefore be identified and quantified. This can be done in many ways, such as by:

■ category of customer;
■ category of product;
■ application introduced – salesforce support, inbound or outbound telemarketing, direct mail and so on;
■ category of change – whether it is cost saving, revenue defence or growth;
■ time period – short, medium or long term;
■ category of staff, function or marketing channel – such as the impact on the field salesforce, sales offices, retail outlets, physical distribution, marketing communication, market research and so on.

Cost-reduction and revenue-increasing effects of some changes are inseparable. If more revenue comes from a fixed cost base, costs fall as a proportion of sales.

The quantification process can be carried out as set out below.

TARGET OPPORTUNITIES

You need to generate a short list of target opportunities for managing customers better. This is usually best achieved in management workshops. This may be supplemented by a series of management interviews and discussions. You may find that many of the best ideas are already present in your company. They may not have been allowed to emerge because of the way in which your policies are planned and implemented. After all, many CRM applications involve using modern information technology to harness the potential of common-sense ideas. They may involve, among other options:

▓ reorganizing work flows or changing the organizational structure and reporting lines;
▓ re-engineering processes;
▓ policy development within existing functions, departments, product groups and so on;
▓ opening up of internal communication channels;
▓ revenue development opportunities;
▓ revenue protection ideas;
▓ quality control measures.

The outcome of this step is a statement of your target opportunities. This provides the focus for the rest of the analysis.

INCREMENTAL REVENUE

Existing marketing plans should be reviewed to identify long-term revenue growth objectives and clarify the basis for plans to achieve these. Revenue growth plans may be based on factors such as overall market growth, specific marketing strategies (product range, price, distribution, advertising and so on) or anticipated competitive changes. Areas to be considered where an improved relationship will make a difference are:

▓ improving retention rates by X per cent – even small percentages may have a very large impact on the bottom line;

■ cross-selling – see how many of your customers buy both product A and product B as, if this percentage is increased, you can usually make substantial additional profits or at least spread marketing and administrative costs over larger revenues;

■ up-selling;

■ improving renewal rates;

■ becoming better at reactivating lapsed customers.

This analysis will indicate the areas where CRM may generate revenue growth by improving the effectiveness of policies that are already planned. Here are some examples of other revenue-generation or protection areas.

Field salesforce and sales office

■ Increased revenue due to the ability of sales staff to concentrate on calling on higher-revenue prospects.

■ Less lost business and fewer lost customers due to improved customer care, as CRM provides improved channels for customers to signal needs.

■ Enhanced new product revenues due to an improved ability to target customers for new products and, eventually, as a result, easier new product launches.

■ Greater ability of the salesforce to handle a broader product portfolio due to the deployment of a response-handling system to inform relevant customers prior to the sales call.

Market research

■ Greater ability to identify the potential for increased revenue among existing customers.

Business and marketing planning

■ More coherent plans to address new revenue opportunities, due to higher quality and relevance of information, leading to higher success rates with launches of new products, greater matching of distribution channels to customer needs and so on.

Retail

■ Ability to market additional products to existing retail customers – whether at retail outlets or by mail order – due to the quality of information about customers.
■ Higher sales volumes of existing products due to an ability to target promotions.

Marketing communications

■ Greater effectiveness of communicating with customers and prospects, leading to higher revenue levels for a given cost.

Product marketing

■ Reduced costs of selling, due to better attunement of channels to customers' needs, leading to the ability to capture higher market share by means of lower prices.

Inventory

■ Reduction in occurrences of stockouts and, therefore, quicker inflow of revenue and reduced loss of sales to competition due to improved sales forecasting.

COST CHANGES

Quantifying the cost savings from implementing CRM prior to implementation is not easy. It is even more difficult if your existing marketing information is not well organized. If you have only recently adhered to the marketing creed, the information required to quantify cost effects may have to be estimated. This may require not only 'reconstruction of figures', based on staff estimates, but the use of pilot studies where particular applications are implemented.

Typically, a comprehensive exercise to gather and analyse cost information is required. It will normally cover every channel of communicating with, and distributing products and services to, customers, such as the salesforce, sales offices operating by telephone and mail, retail outlets, media advertising and direct mail.

The aim is to quantify costs that may be changed by CRM approaches. This exercise is based on interviews, questionnaires and analysis of financial and operating information relating to the channels of communication and distribution. This analysis may have to be carried out by market sector and product line as well as for the whole business, as some of the opportunities may be confined to particular products or sectors. For example, suppose that you need to estimate the cost savings resulting from implementing CRM in relation to a salesforce. The data needed include:

■ salesforce activity analysis, to find out how your sales staff are spending their time – in particular, the time spent on low-productivity activities, such as prospecting and converting low-potential customers, compared with time spent on high-productivity activities, such as converting high-potential customers or preventing their loss;

■ sales revenue productivity statistics, to measure the productivity of the time actually devoted to your customers;

■ data on market size (overall and by product – number of customers and revenue potential), to enable you to estimate the proportion of the market (overall or for given products) left uncovered by your salesforce;

■ data on how the activity profile of your salesforce changes when you implement CRM and put relevant applications (such as telemarketing and direct mail) to work;

■ data on the current costs of managing your salesforce;

■ information on how the activities that generate these costs affect the productivity of your sales staff;

■ information on how CRM disciplines will lead to a change in the nature and scale of these activities (such as data provision work by support staff).

CONTACT STRATEGIES

The current method of contacting customers should be determined. Future contact strategy options, using CRM, should then be identified and an assessment made of:

■ the ability of existing channels to support revenue growth targets and the cost of resourcing those channels to achieve them;

■ the incremental cost of the CRM strategy needed to support the revenue growth target.

With these and other data, cost effects can then be calculated. Consider this business-to-business example. Suppose that a field sales visit costs £250, a highly skilled telephone account management call £8 and a mailing £1 per contact, and the spread of contacts throughout the year is as indicated. In the future strategy, the large (not largest) and medium-sized accounts are responsible for a cost of sales reduction of up to 64 per cent. In the low-volume accounts, although the cost of sales has been increased, at least we are talking to them, giving them the opportunity to identify themselves as potential purchasers. Notice that, in all cases, the number of contacts per year has actually increased. Clearly the measure here will not be just cost of sales, but revenue and customer satisfaction. Some customers will wholeheartedly resist being managed by the telephone, while others will actually welcome it! The key is to identify which ones are which.

Other potential cost-reduction areas are illustrated in the checklist that follows.

Field salesforce

■ Reduction in number needed for given market coverage. This would result from a more efficient calling pattern and less time spent identifying prospects and obtaining prospect information.

■ Reduced staff support required, due to the higher quality of information available to sales staff.

■ Reduced systems support, due to unification of possible variety of support systems.

■ Reduced salesforce turnover due to quality of support and, consequently, greater motivation.

■ Possibly broader span of management control and reduced number of reporting levels feasible. This would be due to a better standard of information on activities and effectiveness of field sales staff, leading to lower management costs.

Sales office

■ Reduced number of staff required to deal with a given number of customers or support a given number of field sales staff. This would be due to a reduction in time spent obtaining and collating information and more efficient prospecting systems.

■ Reduced costs of handling customer enquiries due to improved structuring of the response-handling mechanism, so that customer enquiries go to the relevant destination more smoothly without taking the scenic route.

■ Lower staff turnover due to a higher level of support and, consequently, improved morale.

■ Broader span of control and reduced number of reporting levels feasible, due to a better standard of information on activities and effectiveness of office sales staff, leading to lower management costs.

■ Reduction in the number of branch offices due to the ability to cover the market better and more 'remotely'.

Market research

■ Lower expenditure on external research, due to the higher quality and relevance of information available on customers and prospects.

Marketing and business planning

■ Reduced costs of information collection and management, due to the availability of higher-quality, more relevant and updated information on customers and prospects, leading to a possible reduction in the numbers of planning staff or the planning component of other jobs.

Retail

■ Improved site planning due to the ability to match customer profiles to area profiles more accurately, which might lead to a reduction in the number of outlets to attain given revenue targets.

■ Lower surplus inventory, due to an ability to target 'sale' merchandise marketing.

▓ Greater utilization of space, due to the ability to market special in-store events to database.

Product/brand marketing

▓ Reduced costs of selling, due to better attunement of existing and new channels – some of which are only possible using CRM – to customers' needs.

Marketing communications

▓ Lower costs for achieving any given task, due to greater accountability and the improved ability to identify targets for communication and make communication relevant and, therefore, more effective.

Inventory

▓ Reduced write-offs due to the reduced frequency of launches of inappropriate products and earlier termination of dying products.
▓ General improved forecastability of marketing campaigns, leading to reduced temporary inventory peaks for given products.

REVENUE AND COST REVIEW

A summary of marketing activity over the period of the plan should then be prepared. This should show the effects on costs and revenues of employing existing methods to achieve targets compared with the costs and revenues that should result from the use of CRM. This should show the areas where CRM is more effective.

If the analysis indicates the need for a distribution channel change underpinned by CRM, the result might be a wholesale change in the revenue/cost profile. Whole categories of costs may disappear (as would result from the abolition of sales branches) and new ones appear (such as their replacement by a central sales coordination unit). Changes in distribution channels may create further strategic marketing opportunities, such as the ability to address whole new markets or launch completely different types of products. However, the change may be less revolutionary, such as refocusing a calling salesforce on larger customers and supporting, or even replacing, their efforts by a telemarketing operation.

CRM may afford many opportunities for increasing revenue and reducing costs, but, unless these opportunities are firmly built into operating plans as targets, they are unlikely to be achieved. There needs to be agreement with the appropriate revenue- or cost-responsible functions concerning how revenue and cost opportunities are to be captured. It is therefore important for these functions to be involved in the whole strategic appraisal process.

HOW MUCH TO SPEND

Here, the answer is surprisingly simple – as much as is profitable.

Your research should show you what you risk when CRM fails and what you gain when you get it right. It will also show where the worst problems are and the greatest pay-off is likely to be. It will also show what problems customers face and what needs to be done to resolve them. The next step is the financial calculation – how much extra profit you will make. In some cases, the calculation may look one-sided. This is because you may be forced to improve CRM just to meet competitive standards and stay in business. Therefore, include revenue protection.

Because of interdependence between different CRM activities and the expectations customers may have of continuous improvement, it may be best to develop a long-term programme of development, with recalibration at intervals. This serves to check how customers' needs have changed in the interim and monitor the effectiveness of implementation of your actions.

NEW OPPORTUNITIES FOR IMPROVING CRM

This section should probably be called 'new necessities for improving CRM', at least in competitive markets. This is because low management awareness of the link between CRM, profit and competitiveness implies a poor outlook for companies where CRM standards fall behind those of competitors.

Management awareness that there is a close connection between CRM and profit and that the strength of this connection can be quantified can lead to new approaches to customer management, starting with the identification of groups of customers who wish to be managed differently and ending with a long-term commitment to achieving differentiated and higher levels of CRM in order to maximize profit. The essence of the new approach is a much stronger customer orientation in business and marketing strategy.

FEASIBILITY ANALYSIS

Two constraints that warrant further research are:

▓ technical feasibility;
▓ financial/resource feasibility.

Technical feasibility

Technical feasibility is defined as the levels (frequency, type and quality of contact, planned outcomes) of CRM that it is possible to deliver, at different resource levels. Here, levels of CRM should be translated into likely resulting customer behaviour, as your next step is to work out what levels of CRM it is worth providing, measured against the rewards to you in terms of changed customer behaviour.

Financial feasibility

Once the alternatives that are achievable by means of CRM actions are identified, you are in a position to research their financial feasibility.

CRM is an investment decision like any other and should, therefore, be subject to the same financial disciplines. This should ensure the provision of the right relationship level. It is possible to overinvest in the relationship, with no real return. Assessing financial feasibility requires quantifying the costs of CRM policies and setting them against the benefits (such as reduced future costs of query handling and increased profit as a result of increased sales). This is not always a question of simple calculations. You may have to make assumptions about financial and market factors that will apply in the future. For example, our industrial equipment company will have to make assumptions about:

■ how customers' needs will evolve;
■ what products customers are likely to buy;
■ what the future costs of the provision of CRM are likely to be.

CRM sounds very nice to the marketer, but red lights may flash for your financial management when this term is used, for it can be a bottomless pit for hard-earned money. Hence the need to justify all CRM expenditure in terms of your financial objectives. The best justification for you is increased business from existing customers, reduction in customer losses and more new customers.

CRM does not come in large, indivisible packages. Thus, advocates of increased investment in CRM should be asked to justify not only the whole package, but every individual element of it. This is the only way to stop the building in of unnecessary costs.

The main types of costs involved in setting up CRM include:

■ systems – hardware, software development and/or licences, telecommunications;
■ training of specific people, including time off territory;
■ culture shift education programmes for the organization;
■ process re-engineering;
■ policy development, in terms of the time this takes;
■ setting up new units – such as telemarketing units;
■ closure of old units – such as branches;
■ redundancy payments.

These must be set against the marketing benefits. These lie principally in the areas of customer acquisition and retention. Your ability to acquire and retain customers is critically dependent on how well you satisfy their needs – the subject of the next chapter.

6

Identifying Customers' Relationship Needs

THE TEN KEY QUESTIONS

The key questions you face in deciding what approach to take in CRM are the following.

1. With which customers do you want to create and manage a relationship?
2. What are these customers' behaviours, needs and perceptions?
3. What is their relative importance – for example, do they constitute a hierarchy?
4. How far do your policies meet their needs today?
5. What are the other relevant offerings you should position yours to compete against?
6. What are your customers' experiences of your products, services and the relationship as a whole?
7. What does your staff believe about its role in your relationship with customers?
8. What do commercial indicators of relationship success show – brand loyalty, market share?
9. Can your customers be grouped into coherent segments, to enable CRM policy to be structured to meet their needs?
10. What are these segments, and are they stable?

THE RESEARCH PROCESS AND THE POLICY PROCESS

Clearly, many of the answers should be sought from customers. You can't build a relationship without talking to the other party first! The *research* process should be integrated closely with the *policy* process. Information is not being gathered for the sake of it, but to influence policy. This means that the content, coverage and timing of research should be integrated within the planning process. To ensure this, each piece of research should:

■ have specific objectives;
■ improve the quality of the next piece of research;
■ have clear policy outcomes.

WHAT IS THE POLICY PROCESS?

The conventional policy process works for CRM just as well as it does for any other area of decision making. This process consists of:

■ **research and analysis** to identify what is possible and what customers need, covering the product and service portfolio, relationship standards and customers' behaviour;
■ **determination of objectives, policies and main projects** to ensure that the policies required to meet customers' needs are adopted;
■ **agreement on the details of policies and implementation projects** to ensure delivery of the policies;
■ **measurement and control** to ensure that your policies are properly implemented and the need for any modifications picked up.

This policy process must include the following.

■ How your CRM will cause it to stand out from that offered by other suppliers – whether they are directly or indirectly competitive or just suppliers whose standards of CRM are likely to provide a basis for comparison. This answers the

question 'How well should you be perceived to be performing when compared to other suppliers?' This is defined as
competitiveness.

■ What should be done to ensure that your customers' needs are
met – that is, the answers to the questions 'What does the
customer want to happen in their relationship with you?' and
'What does the supplier want to happen so that these
customers' needs are met?' These are defined as **relationship
performance requirements**.

RESEARCHING COMPETITIVE REQUIREMENTS

Competitive CRM performance must be researched and assessed.
This immediately raises the question as to who should be regarded
as competition. The answer to this lies mainly with customers,
who have their own basis for comparison, so it is enough to ask
them.

Where direct competitors are absent or are not very large or
effective, consumers may choose 'parallel' organizations – those
they see as involved in similar activities or as similarly large. Thus,
telecommunications may be compared with other utilities – gas,
water and electricity. However, utilities may be compared to
retailers, as the latter provide most consumers with their
commonest experience of interaction with large commercial organizations.

As usual, we need to distinguish between what CRM competitors *are* delivering and what customers *perceive* them to be
delivering.

What's being delivered today

Customers' perceptions of what is being delivered are, of course,
determined partly by what your competitors actually deliver. This,
in turn, is partly determined by the policies they have in place to
deliver it. Obviously, it is not always possible to get detailed information on competitive policies. Strategies for doing this include:

■ direct formal or informal exchange of information with
competitors, which is most feasible when:

- competition is indirect;
- their top management does not see CRM as a major factor in overall competitive success;
- competitors have to work together on specific customer projects (industrial equipment suppliers often have to);
▓ hiring competitive staff;
▓ briefing market research agencies to collect data, which can be done in the following ways:
- agencies interviewing competitive staff;
- using agencies to set up 'multi-client studies' in which competitors pool information on an anonymous basis;
▓ experiencing CRM – by becoming a customer of the company concerned.

Ask the following kinds of questions to examine particular issues of importance to this aspect of CRM.

▓ How reliable is the delivery of CRM – is it variable in quality, timing and so on?
▓ What channels or media are used to manage customers?
▓ What does the delivery depend on? Is it systems, processes or simply personal initiative of the staff?
▓ How much does it cost to deliver it? Figures may need to be based on informed guesses about the kinds of policies, procedures and resources that are being used to deliver CRM.
▓ What benefits does the competitor derive from it? Information on this may be derived from market research on customer loyalty.

The competitive future

Researching the current competitive position is not enough. Relying solely on today's information would lead to CRM policies being designed to meet past requirements and situations. Therefore, you need to:

▓ examine past trends in competitive policies;
▓ try to assess how your competitors are thinking about this area;
▓ examine any information you have about their recruitment of staff or suppliers likely to be involved in developing CRM.

RELATIONSHIP PERFORMANCE REQUIREMENTS

The most important activity in researching customer relationship needs is to define customers' general perceptions, wants and expectations regarding the relationship. This means finding answers to the questions in the checklist in Figure 6.1.

Which performance requirements do you know now or need to research?	Know now	Research
▓ What are the principal dimensions which customers use to measure relationship performance (eg information exchanged, long- and short-term benefits of the relationship, contact frequency, speed of query or complaint resolution, staff behaviour)?		
▓ How do customers perceive current levels of performance?		
▓ When do customers believe that the relationship starts, and, within it, transactions and contact episodes?		
▓ What are the minimum levels of relationship achievement that customers will tolerate while staying loyal?		
▓ What is the maximum level of relationship management that customers believe that it would be reasonable for you to supply?		
▓ What are the main areas where customers see the need for improvement?		
▓ How strongly do customers feel about relationship performance?		
▓ How important is the relationship in customers' decisions to buy the core product or service?		
▓ Where does the customer wish the locus of control of the relationship to be?		
▓ What changes in all the above are likely to occur during the period for which policy is being made? What will cause these changes (eg economic, social or demographic factors, competitive actions)?		
▓ What image of you would the customer like to have?		
▓ Is it possible to identify particular groups of customers with significantly different relationship requirements?		
▓ If there is a risk of certain types of customers not being 'right' for you in some way, what reasons for your refusing to do business with them will be accepted by these customers?		

Figure 6.1 *Checklist for research*

The above information relates to what customers need in the way of relationship. To this must be added information on:

▨ what relationship is actually achieved, as perceived by both customer and supplier;
▨ what changes are planned in relationship management.

The result of the above analysis should be a comparison between current and planned levels of relationship management and customers' needs. This will be fed into the next stage of the process.

THE CONTACT AUDIT

You need to understand how the different contacts a customer has with you affect customers' attitudes and perceptions concerning the relationship. The contact audit begins by identifying all the contact points. The audit shows the type, nature, frequency and quality of contact with customers. It should also show how these contacts affect customers' perceptions and attitudes. You may be surprised – as many managers are – to find just how many points of contact exist between your organization and your customers.

MAKING SENSE OF CUSTOMER DATA

Except in the smallest organization, CRM policies cannot be completely tailored to the needs of individual customers. If you have very high-quality information about customers, do not mistake the ability to identify differences in relationship needs at the individual level for the ability to deliver different relationships. You will almost certainly need to group customers. The most relevant way to group them is according to their attitudes and likely responses to CRM policies.

The importance of segmentation

'Segmentation' is just another word for putting customers into groups sharing similar characteristics that affect their behaviour in the market (buying, media and so on). Segmentation is used for the following reasons.

■ It gives you a better basis for understanding the whole market. Even if you market the same product or service to segments that behave differently, you will understand the whole market better if you know how different segments of it behave. However, if the relationship is an important part of a complicated product/service offering, then it is possible to adjust the relationship to suit different types of customers, while maintaining the same core offer.

■ If different segments respond differently to marketing policy, and if policies can be attuned to different segments, you can achieve your objectives more easily than if you follow an undifferentiated policy (one policy applied to the whole market). If the relationship needs of different kinds of customers differ quite radically, then the total product/service offering may be differentiated purely or mainly in terms of the relationship offered.

■ Segmentation can bring benefits of focus, concentration, specialization and, hence, differentiation. These benefits include increased profits or sales, lower costs and prevention of competitive entry. This is because a focused marketing policy makes you very good at meeting the needs of your chosen segment(s). If the relationship needs of each segment are analysed in depth, you are in a strong position to fine-tune your relationship offering so as to meet the needs of your chosen segment.

CRM policies can be anything from very general, which are those that are applicable to the whole market, to highly differentiated, which involve different procedures being followed for different kinds of customers and situations. If you want to meet the needs of many different types of customers, you can opt for a core relationship offering with 'add-ons' that are targeted at specific segments.

TAKING THE CUSTOMER INTO ACCOUNT

The above analysis shows that your customers cannot be treated like one-dimensional objects. Each customer is a complicated mix of personality, motivations, attitudes and needs, preferring particular kinds of experiences and learning from them. CRM policy must take this into account. Obviously, you cannot have a deep understanding of every customer. However, you must understand customers' perspectives in order to be able to meet their needs.

The demand for attention

Customers have some idea of the kinds and levels of relationships they want or do not want. Between neglect and an over-attentive relationship lie all kinds of possibilities. How can you possibly allow for the wide range of requirements that your customers might have? The answer to this lies in the many different ways in which you can differentiate the relationship. These include:

■ giving information – about products, services, current status of the relationship, how your customers can access you, how they can get more information, different ways of paying, how to set up different kinds of relationship;
■ obtaining information about the customers' needs – what they need, when, how;
■ giving a commitment to supply;
■ gaining a commitment to buy;
■ providing reassurance;
■ helping customers buy or use to obtain maximum benefit;
■ improving the service.

PLANNING THE RELATIONSHIP

Customers will require different levels of attention in all the ways listed above. Meeting the right combination of needs is easier the earlier in your business planning process you start your relationship planning. You need to:

■ decide with which customers a relationship is to be created;
■ research and model their needs;
■ determine the type and level of relationship to be provided in order to meet both customers' needs and suppliers' objectives;
■ build flexibility into your relationship delivery system so you can meet individual variations within general requirements.

CHOOSING CUSTOMERS

Not every supplier has the luxury of being able to choose customers. For example, public utilities and retailers must normally do business with any customer who comes along, no matter how problematical or litigious they are. However, the issue is not simply one of what customers can do in principle. Rather, it is a question of which of these customers are most encouraged to buy. Branding, marketing communications, store layout, pricing, product range and all the other items of the marketing mix can attract particular kinds of customers while others can be deterred. For example, retail customers requiring a very close relationship may understand from the layout and staffing of a self-service store and the absence of any loyalty or store card scheme that they are unlikely to meet their needs in such a store. In a department store, the layout, numbers of assistants and the existence of a combined store card and loyalty scheme give a different message.

A key principle of CRM is that it is hard to meet all your customers' needs all of the time. It is therefore essential to prioritize customers and needs. Competitive survival is achieved by meeting the most important needs of the most important customers. Competitive advantage is obtained by doing this *and* meeting the needs of customers whose needs are not being met by competitive providers.

For this reason, you must:

■ have a good understanding of the needs of different groups of customers;
■ prioritize customers and needs.

However, there is a decision that needs to be made first – with which groups of customers to create a relationship.

THE IDEA OF STRATEGIC SEGMENTATION

You should find the following hierarchy of segmentation helpful in the targeting process.

Analytical segmentation

Here, you need information on customers and markets to identify that you do have different groups of customers with different profiles, needs and so on. You start with very broad questions, such as 'What kinds of customers do I have, how do they behave, which products or channels are the most successful at managing them?' The segments that you identify in this way may never be subjected to different promotions, policies or strategies. For example, you may aggregate them into a target market for a promotion. The main criterion for successful use of analytical segmentation is that any resulting strategies work overall because they are based on in-depth understanding of customers' needs. Analytical segmentation often provides the foundation for the other three types of segmentation.

Response segmentation

Here, you identify different groups of customers to target particular promotions at. A given customer may belong to a whole series of different segments, according to the objectives of individual promotions. The key success criterion for response segmentation is how well each of your promotions does – that is, whether or not your response rates met expectations, final purchases hit your targets and so on.

Strategic segmentation

For this type of segmentation, you identify groups of customers who need to be handled differently in some way. For example, mass-market financial services suppliers need to identify:

■ loan customers who are likely to be higher credit risks – in which case, they are usually only accepted as borrowers at an interest rate that covers the risk premium;
■ mortgage customers who are likely to be rapid switchers (to competitors' mortgages), in which case they may only be accepted for loans with higher penalties for early cancellation;
■ conversely, low-risk customers or those who switch infrequently will be targeted and marketed to intensively, and particular attention might be paid to the quality of the relationship established with them.

The idea of strategic segmentation is to ensure that each of your actual or potential customers is allocated, at a minimum, to at least one strategic category – membership of which carries certain implications for your marketing policy towards them. You must avoid creating too many categories, with attendant risks of both overlap (a given customer being subjected to too many marketing initiatives or restrictions, which have to be resolved by prioritization rules) and of over-complexity (because of the number of segments that need to be addressed with different marketing policies). A particular issue of importance for both strategic and loyalty segmentation is the movement of customers between categories.

Delivered loyalty segmentation

This is a special case of strategic segmentation. Here, you identify particular groups of actual or potential customers whose loyalty is critical to you. They are usually critical to you in terms of the volume and profitability of business they bring, but other variables (such as political sensitivity) can also come into play. Identification of this group is followed by the development and implementation, or 'delivery', of a practical marketing approach, including branding, relationship management (by means of whichever channels are appropriate), promotional management and systems support. This works to draw that group of customers into a special, long-standing, mutually committed and transcending relationship with you.

The actual components of delivered loyalty segmentation are usually no different from ordinary loyalty programmes. What is different, though, is the focus of your organization on that segment and commitment of resources to managing it profitably and well. Perhaps the most important feature of such segmentation is the degree of commitment of the organization to the segment. If it is to work, your organization must have fully committed to the segmentation approach.

The systems and management characteristics of these four kinds of segmentation are summarized in Table 6.1.

Table 6.1 *Systems and management requirements for different approaches to segmentation*

	Analytical	Response	Strategic	Loyalty
Technical approach	Can be left to expert systems and datamining approaches.	Expert/datamining approaches may be used, but test results are key.	In-depth business understanding required to define issue.	In-depth business understanding required to define issue.
Senior management involvement	Not required, except to ensure that ability exists.	Required if promotions are a large share of marketing budget.	Important in defining areas of strategic focus.	Absolutely critical because of subsequent commitment to comprehensive loyalty management approach.
Customer contact implications	Depends on conclusion.	Customers experience correctly defined and targeted promotions.	Customers may be required to give more information and should find that they are being offered more appropriate products and services.	Customers who are loyal, or who have the propensity to be so, experience more integrated management, whatever the contact point and whatever the product or service.

RESEARCHING AND MODELLING NEEDS

Many suppliers make the mistake of amassing large amounts of data on customers' needs. This data – not surprisingly – usually shows that:

▧ customers have a great variety of needs;
▧ these needs influence customers' buying behaviour in all sorts of ways.

It is therefore essential for you to try to develop a model of customers' behaviour, how it affects your customers' relationship requirements and how achieving that relationship creates business success. Having such a model is key if relationship needs are to influence policy.

DETERMINING RELATIONSHIP TYPES AND LEVELS

Once you have identified the broad relationship requirements of your target customers by means of research, the next step is to determine target levels and the type of relationship they will respond to best. You need to decide where on the spectrum of relationship management – between neglect and an intense relationship – the customer wishes to be.

Given that relationship requirements are dependent on the types of customers concerned and the needs of the moment, exact positioning of the group of target customers will not be possible. You must therefore determine the base level of the relationship that should be provided. Variations around this level must be achieved either by contractual variations or by flexibility of relationship delivery. You should determine the base level of the relationship on strategic, competitive grounds, as an important component of marketing strategy. Likely variations in requirements should be analysed and grouped, so that meeting them can be done without the need for too complicated a process. There should also be frequent feedback from customers about their perceptions and attitudes towards the relationship. In this way, you will ensure that broad policies are correct and that, at the front line, the right attunement to individual needs is taking place.

BUILDING IN FLEXIBILITY

The larger the organization, the more difficult it seems to be to remain flexible to customers' needs. You therefore need to allow your staff some flexibility. For example, if a customer asks for a particular delivery date, the person receiving the call can give a precise response if scheduling information has been provided on-line. If your information systems are not capable of delivering this kind of information, then some leeway may be given to the person receiving the call to reduce that customer's uncertainty about delivery dates by making it possible for them to call the customer back to confirm a date and time.

Flexibility is a key attribute of CRM. However, even the best planning and information systems cannot deliver the quality of relationship that a highly motivated individual, supported by well-planned processes and systems and operating within clear guidelines, can – staff are very important too.

USING MARKET RESEARCH WISELY

A key aspect of the information systems used in planning and managing CRM is market research. In the next chapter, we explain the special market research disciplines you need for CRM.

7

The Role of Market Research

'If you can't measure it, you can't manage it' is one of those nicely turned phrases that sounds so obvious that you might wonder why anyone bothered to say it. Of course, it's not even true – many good managers work by feel and produce better results than their peers who feel exposed without measurement. This is even true of CRM, where a policy of 'staying close to customers', and ensuring that staff members do the same, can be just as effective as measurement-driven management.

Yet, measurement has its place – particularly in large, complicated businesses or ones where it is difficult to gain perspective on how customers feel about the relationship. So, how should you go about it?

WHAT ARE YOU TRYING TO MEASURE?

If you're trying to find out whether or not your customers are happy about their relationship with you, then it makes sense to define the scope of any research as how a customer might perceive the relationship as well as what they might feel about it. We suggest this definition:

How customers define and perceive their relationship with you, overall and particularly during any period in which those customers believe that they are in transaction with you.

It is normally easier to measure just at the point when the relationship with the organization is consummated – the 'moment of truth'. Yet, the reality of most customer relationships is that this moment is preceded by a period of anticipated contact and followed by reflection. Their attitude to you is formed over a long period and can change while other contacts, or attempts at contact, can be made. Here are some examples of such events:

◼ dialling a Freephone number and receiving the engaged tone;
◼ trying to fix an appointment with the bank manager;
◼ browsing in a car showroom but not talking to the salesperson;
◼ visiting a clothes store and leaving without purchasing anything.

The transaction may be of various kinds – sales, service, payment, seeking information and so on. However, whatever it is, our first step in research is to find out what the perceived relationship and, within it, the perceived transaction period, are for different types of customers and relationships.

INTERNAL AND EXTERNAL MEASURES

The larger your company, the harder it is for your management to understand all your customers' needs and perceptions, and the more remote they are likely to be from customer contact staff (though this depends on the nature of your business and, in particular, whether the relationship is delivered by people or equipment, such as self-service arrangements and computers).

Whatever the situation, however, you need both a quantitative and qualitative understanding of customers' relationship perceptions and preferences – from the point of view of the company as a whole and from that of your front-line customer-facing staff. This gives you the basis for complete customer management and understanding. Also, a consistent research and measurement initiative demonstrates management's desire to do more than evangelize.

PART OF THE RELATIONSHIP

If you are planning to base your relationship management decisions on measurement, you need to understand that interaction with customers is not an 'arm's length' exercise. Often, make or break events happen when you and your customers are closely involved with each other, customers often doing their part to create or consummate the relationship. So, you should focus on the transactions themselves, your customers and their overall relationship with you, including how long the relationship has been established, how well it has gone in the past and their feelings about the relationship. In particular, you must take into account issues such as:

■ how customers can become emotionally attached to, or irritated by, particular transactions within an otherwise good relationship, perhaps as delivered by particular individuals;
■ how branding, product range and customer loyalty affects customers' perceptions of the relationship and what they will say to you;
■ how slowly customers' attitudes to the overall relationship – including their loyalty to a company – evolve;
■ how, when your customers' attitudes do evolve, this changes their attitudes to individual transactions within the relationship, including the slightly paradoxical fact that loyal customers are often the most difficult to manage, because they have higher expectations of the relationship than those new to the company;
■ whether customers feel in some way dependent on you or wish to be strongly in control, and how this might affect what they say about you.

WHAT TECHNIQUES ARE AVAILABLE?

In this brief chapter, we cannot cover all possible techniques in detail. In fact, the techniques are all part of the standard market research repertoire, so here we focus on what you can and can't do with some of the most commonly used techniques. These include:

▓ desk research
▓ qualitative groups
▓ quantitative research
▓ Web and e-mail questionnaires
▓ telephone questionnaires
▓ mystery shopping
▓ competitive research
▓ internal audit
▓ user groups
▓ customer feedback
▓ staff research.

Desk research

Reports on previous studies of customers' needs and how they are met are particularly valuable. They show the variety of customers' needs, but also indicate how these needs can be grouped and what sorts of policies have been used to meet them.

Qualitative groups

With this technique, small groups of customers – selected according to a detailed profile – spend an hour or more with an experienced researcher discussing specific relationship and service issues and responding to pre-defined statements. Properly used – that is, with participants properly selected and the discussion conducted by a professional researcher and reported comprehensively – groups will give you a detailed understanding of how a cross-section of customers feel about these issues. They also offer an opportunity to deal with anecdotal evidence in a positive and constructive way. If you are in a hurry to confirm an idea or diagnose a problem, groups probably provide the quickest turnaround time – often as little as two to three weeks. An additional benefit is that groups give customers a warm feeling that you really care and want to listen to their views – a feeling that is enhanced by their receiving payment for participation or, better, gifts of your products or services.

However, groups only give you the views of a few people – tens rather than the hundreds or thousands needed for a representative sample. Therefore, they won't:

▓ give you a continuous audit of standards and trends in their achievement;

▓ provide a benchmark against which to set relationship management standards.

Groups may not be popular with staff if their positive benefits are not sold properly. Researching individual customers is one thing, getting them together to talk about your company and (as staff may see it) their role in it is another, so staff sometimes do resist helping recruit customers.

Quantitative research

This involves running detailed questionnaires on many respondents. Questionnaires are usually structured – that is, with carefully formulated questions, mostly requiring specific answers, although room may be left for a broader range of responses. In some cases, such as for senior decision makers buying business services, questionnaires may be unstructured, with the interviewer working through a checklist of more open-ended questions. Questionnaire design is usually based on the results of group research – the latter being used to identify the language your customers use to talk about you, the relationship you provide and their key concerns.

This approach should be used if you want a large enough sample to derive a statistically valid result. If qualitative information is required, this can be elicited by asking consumers more detailed questions about why they respond in particular ways to particular questions. Mailed questionnaires have the following advantages:

▓ they are more economical and convenient than personal interviews;

▓ they avoid interviewer bias;

▓ they give people time to consider their answers;

▓ they can be anonymous;

and these disadvantages:

▓ the questions need to be very straightforward if the response is to be valid;

▓ answers must be taken as final;

- respondents see the whole questionnaire before answering it;
- it is impossible to be sure that the right person answers it;
- many recipients may not respond;
- non-response may lead to bias in results, because those not responding are different in some way from those responding – for example, they may be less loyal customers;
- the higher the response rate, the more valid the result – but the only way to check this is by chasing up a sample of responders.

The response rate can be increased by:

- enclosing a covering letter explaining what the survey is trying to achieve, how the respondent's name was selected and why the recipient should reply;
- telling the respondent the benefits of replying;
- explaining why the survey is important;
- enclosing a stamped, addressed or business reply envelope;
- giving a premium for responding;
- following up.

If the questionnaire is properly designed and administered regularly to a representative sample of customers, quantitative research will give a detailed and continuing view of:

- perceptions – what relationship customers think they are actually in;
- satisfaction levels – how satisfied they are with it;
- tolerance – what service levels customers will tolerate within the relationship and what levels they won't;
- desires – what customers would really like and, where relevant, what they'd be prepared to sacrifice to obtain it, such as price, user costs and so on.

Analysis of responses will also show how these are related to each other and should provide the key to:

- relationship design, when analysed together with customer characteristics and 'grossed up' to provide a picture of service demand for the whole market;
- standard setting.

Research aimed at determining customers' satisfaction levels should aim not only to find out levels of satisfaction, but also causes of variations over time and between branches, individuals and so on.

In service industries, where the research is just required to monitor achievement of relationship management standards, use of self-completion questionnaires, administered by point-of-contact staff, can demonstrate management's trust in these staff and secure their involvement. However, care must be taken to monitor possible bias because of customers' desire to please or punish the individual staff member who has served them. In some cases, anonymity is also critical. In the best of all worlds – where staff are totally responsible and service levels and outcomes are measurable in hard business terms, such as sales and profit – staff can run the system, use the results and relay them to a wider audience. This can lead to a nearly ideal mix of staff involvement, customer satisfaction and profit.

However, questionnaires will not give in-depth views of the emotion that lies behind decisions and complaints.

If your business is one in which customer data is hard to come by and you are keen to use database marketing techniques, a customer questionnaire is one of the best ways of gathering data – not only on customer attitudes towards the service, but also on the customers themselves and how they use the service. Airlines are one of the best examples of this use.

Web and e-mail questionnaires

These are becoming increasingly popular, as they allow customers to enter data in a structured way. They are particularly valuable if customers are validated (for example, by account number), as then you know who the feedback is coming from (not just anybody). Also, having structured questionnaires on the Web prevents the problem of high volumes of amorphous feedback.

Such e-mail questionnaires are also very useful in business-to-business research, when you are aiming to find out about a small number of customers in depth and open-ended responses are permitted.

Telephone questionnaires

These are used in very similar contexts to mail questionnaires, with the notable addition of questionnaires administered when customers call in to respond to a promotion. Telephone surveys are normally more accurate than mail surveys and combine many of the advantages of mail questionnaires and in-depth interviews in that:

■ they are private;
■ they are one to one;
■ the consumers cannot see the whole questionnaire and so they focus on each question as it comes;
■ any problems of understanding can be dealt with;
■ careful scripting helps avoid interview bias;
■ computerized routeing of questionnaires allows for complicated patterns of behaviour to be captured;
■ response rates are higher – customers can be called until they reply;
■ costs are lower than for personal interviews;
■ the telephone is a way of life to business;
■ speed – telephones get higher priority than post and the results are immediately available.

The disadvantages of them are that:

■ some consumers object to the approach;
■ the costs of setting up a telephone questionnaire can be high;
■ calling costs are higher than postal costs;
■ it is a voice medium only, so customers' reactions cannot be seen.

In telephone, postal or face-to-face interviewing, there is now much accumulated expertise concerning how to design questionnaires to elicit CRM needs and attitudes. The recommendations arising from this experience can be summarized as follows:

■ do not rely on satisfaction ratings alone – these may give a useful idea of the extent to which customers are satisfied with the relationship, but do not give a good indication of specific requirements, so questions should be oriented to identifying specific needs;

■ customers have many needs, so it is important not to try to condense them into a few simple questions – it is usually a good idea to carry out a few in-depth interviews or group discussions to identify the variety of needs, then design the questionnaire with as many questions as are needed to cover these needs;

■ questions should be as specific as possible – general questions bring imprecise answers that are not so immediately actionable as more specific information;

■ the reliability of answers should be cross-checked, by asking the same question in different ways and possibly by combining postal, telephone and face-to-face interviewing to check consistency across the different techniques;

■ if comments are asked for (often at the end of the questionnaire), they should be requests for specific recommendations, such as improvements to particular aspects of particular services – again, general comments have little value.

Mystery shopping

This is a very popular service research technique, particularly among companies that make their service available via a large number of outlets (their own or dealers) or staff (such as telephone-based services). This includes not just true service industries, but also suppliers of manufactured goods where the buyer would not be identifiable by name. It is more difficult to use this technique in industrial goods markets, except those served by distributors, because in the former it is normal to ask for customers' details before handling problems.

This technique involves external staff posing as customers and then rating the service they receive using a form. The approach should be used only after careful planning and consultation with staff, and with a clear policy output that is known to and understood by staff – whether this be a competition or a service policy improvement. Results should be published as soon as possible after the audit, in a non-confrontational, positive way, with the offer of training and resources to remedy any problems highlighted by the audit. This implies that a budget should be set aside for this remedial work (a rough guide is to budget ten times as much for improvement as for research).

Competitive research

This is vital. As we stressed in the last chapter, using CRM competitively requires knowledge of how competitors are treating their customers as well as what they are doing to achieve their relationships. Some information on this can be gathered from customers using the techniques mentioned above. However, experiencing competitive relationships is vital. This is parallel to the manufacturing practice of buying competitive products and stripping them down to find out how they are made, how reliable they are and what they can do. To experience the relationship, competitive programmes should be subscribed to and individual components of the relationship tested – for example, calling customer helplines. Finally, it is important to try to envisage what competitors' own CRM strategies are likely to be.

Internal audit

This involves auditing the relationship as delivered, rather than as perceived by customers. In many cases, audit data is reported by staff or automated computer systems, such as the time taken to answer the telephone, percentages of calls connected, percentages of trains/flights arriving on time, percentages of calls/contacts where customers' relationships with the company are not accurately identified. Auditing may be undertaken prior to other forms of research to identify the 'reality' customers are faced with and, after setting standards based on the quantitative research, determine whether or not standards are being met. You may wish to incorporate the standard into a customers' charter, in which case you will need to audit frequently.

User groups

These exist mainly in business-to-business markets, particularly for services and products that are very important to customers, such as information technology. They are so important as a source of feedback to suppliers that they are often funded by them. They may also conduct their own surveys of their members. As a general feedback mechanism, they are excellent. Indeed, there is much research to show that some of the most successful products and services – particularly in business-to-business markets – are derived from customers' ideas. They also represent an excellent forum in which to test ideas for new products and services. However, they can represent something of a vested interest, particularly if they are dominated by a few big users, so you should take care to ensure representativeness. Where this is difficult, it may be better to sponsor the formation of separate associations or at least separate sections of the main association.

Customer feedback

This was once the most neglected form of research. It was often treated as 'complaints'. The information arising from complaints was used to rectify the situation the customer was complaining about. Perhaps letters with compliments were passed to the appropriate staff, but the rest of the information was lost. This led to a vicious circle. Customers viewed giving feedback as pointless because they received no acknowledgement and saw no results in company policy. Staff failed to pass feedback on. This was because they saw no actions resulting from their efforts and the 'shoot the messenger' syndrome was present.

An additional point to bear in mind is that customer behaviour lags behind changes in levels of satisfaction or emotion. For example, a customer who, for many years, has been satisfied with the relationship with a particular supplier will go on buying from that customer for a time after the relationship starts to deteriorate and may not complain for a while. Alternatively, they may complain immediately, but not become disloyal, so their complaint may be ignored because the feeling is 'they'll stick with us anyway', or 'they weren't really serious'. Conversely, when matters improve, it may take time for customers to experience the improvement, so they may not return or increase their purchasing/loyalty for some time. This can lead staff to become indifferent about customer feedback as they do not see the immediate effect of it in company performance.

However, today, many large companies realize that improving the relationship provides good long-term benefits. They are deploying a variety of techniques to channel customer feedback into points where it can be dealt with quickly and effectively and used to produce information to steer policy.

Positive handling of your customers' complaints wins points

with customers and makes them recommend you – sometimes even more than if you had satisfied them in the first instance! This may be because it's only when they complain that you give them attention – a dangerous situation. However, using complaints and other customer-originated comments, such as suggestions for improvements, as a measurement is not advisable unless you have left no stone unturned in ensuring that your customers can express their feelings to you when they want.

There is much research to show that the vast majority of customers don't express their feelings voluntarily to suppliers. Most customers who wish to complain will do so to their friends and colleagues, possibly dissuading them from using the service. Only very satisfied or loyal customers will take the time to write or call. Techniques used to overcome these barriers to customer feedback include:

■ distributing feedback forms (note, not complaint forms), giving customers an incentive to complete them and staff an incentive to ensure that they are completed, such as during service provision at payment time;
■ incorporating feedback routines into other documentation routines, such as delivery notes, receipts, boarding documents, club membership mailings and so on;
■ setting up an inbound telemarketing facility to handle calls and promoting the number widely;
■ calling customers after they have received service.

The more you can pre-structure feedback using these techniques, the easier it is for you to analyse and the greater your opportunity of collecting other data from your customers at the same time.

If your company is very large, the volume of customer feedback may be large enough to justify setting up a specialist customer relations department to handle it. In such cases, classification of feedback into different categories can provide useful evidence of the company's success in meeting customers' requirements.

Complaints and compliments are very destructive if they are used by themselves to reward or punish staff as they can obviously be manipulated – customers, too, may find they are put under pressure to 'accentuate the positive and eliminate the negative'. The key here is also to separate the complaint from the complainer and satisfy the complainer while recording the complaint and dealing with the root cause.

Staff research

If your relationship with customers depends on your staff, the latter's attitudes and opinions should also be researched. This is usually done using questionnaires and focus groups, as with consumers. The aim is to uncover the real truth about the front line. Front-line staff face both ways, and staff workshops will quickly reveal what barriers they face to improving the relationship with your customers. They will also reveal if what you are trying to do is inconsistent with the prevalent culture. For example, if you're trying to improve customer loyalty, you need to ensure that staff themselves are loyal and understand the importance of loyalty. If staff turnover is high, you need very strong incentives and people-management processes to get staff to focus on longer-term management of customers. However, if your sole objective is to serve customers quickly, the effect of high staff turnover can be managed.

Don't be surprised if staff tell you in workshops that most of the problems lie in the way that you have designed their jobs, recruited, trained and managed them. They'll be right – probably because you haven't designed good customer management processes. The workshops will also reveal where staff need new ideas, training, improved communication and coaching on how to use their existing skills better. They will also reveal where you've recruited the wrong types of people.

In conducting staff research, you need to take into account the views of local management. Many on-site managers are problem-solvers, diving in to sort out problems, then jumping out to sort out problems elsewhere, even thriving on crisis – it makes them feel wanted. The vision you're painting is one in which things run smoothly. Thus, they may not like this and resist the whole process of taking staff opinion into account. However, line managers' roles can be structured much better if you design your customer management processes and staff roles around managing customers, put measurement and systems in place to spot problems early, and get managers to deal with the cause rather than the outcome – a fundamental quality principle.

USING THE RESULTS

As with all market research, it is important to allocate the time and money to digest the findings, identify policy conclusions and implement them. You do need to ensure that staff members are involved in this process, just as they should be involved in the research. One approach in larger companies is to use review boards, composed of local staff, who review 'their' results against those of other branches and derive their own conclusions.

INTERPRETING THE RESULTS

Interpreting relationship management research is not always straightforward. For example, customers who are satisfied when they transact with you won't necessarily rebuy, because satisfaction with the relationship measures only one issue – for example, it ignores the intrinsic quality of the product. So, research should always include an element that allows analysis of the connection between attitudes towards the relationship and customers' buying behaviour. Only when this has been done is it advisable to set standards.

COMPETITIVE STANDARDS

Standards should also take into account any relevant competitive benchmarks, so attitudes to relationships with competitive companies should also have been measured. As we stressed in the last chapter, a pre-condition for this is determining which companies are considered by customers to be relevant competitors and in which respects.

It is also as well to bear in mind what a reasonable standard should be. It is no use setting unattainable standards, even if they are based on research, as this would be very demotivating for staff. The appropriate policy is therefore to raise standards slowly, as the policies designed to achieve these improvements are implemented. Don't expect that just by setting higher standards you'll achieve long-term improvement – what you'll get is a short-term boost to performance, possibly followed by an increase in staff attrition rates.

So, pacing your improvement is vital. We suggest that if your research shows you're behind your competitors, you should identify the most serious areas of weakness and focus on them, gradually bringing your performance up to par with them. Once you're there, you can focus on getting ahead. The only exception to this is if you believe that a complete re-engineering of how you manage customer relationships will allow you to leapfrog your competitors.

As your business will continue to serve its customers, it should also continue to research them. The culture of listening to customers will only take root if staff members at all levels are involved in the process of listening, interpreting and then making the changes customers require.

IS IT WORTH RESEARCHING?

The answer to this question depends on what you're going to do with the research. Normally, the answer is 'only if you're going to manage and improve relationships with customers'. This in turn depends on the corporate benefit. In competitive markets, asking this question may be unnecessary, as failure to focus by measuring may cause general failure with customers.

Responding to measurement requires management of budgets, overtime, staff turnover (the loyalty culture), revenue and loyalty schemes and, where the relationship is delivered via automated or semi-automated approaches, reconsideration of systems strategies. For example, if you're not prepared to respond fully, then a full measurement programme may not be appropriate. However, you may need to carry out a full measurement at least once to demonstrate to senior management the effects of good CRM.

INTEGRATING THE RESEARCH

All the above sources of information should be integrated with the results of other kinds of feedback from customers. Staff feedback should also be used, as it is critical to get staff views on what is happening to the relationship between you and your customers and what you are doing to help your staff improve it.

READY TO DEVELOP THE RELATIONSHIP

With your customers well researched and understood, you're now ready to embark on the difficult process of acquiring and retaining customers – the subject of the rest of this book.

8

Customer Retention and Loyalty

STRATEGIC CRM

CRM has often been labelled as an operational tactic because many of its disciplines derive from direct marketing and, even more specifically, from direct mail.

Its use at the business and, indeed, corporate level of strategy planning is relatively new and, as yet, not universally accepted. The key aspect of CRM is the ability to collect, analyse and track customer information. This information on your database is a corporate planning asset. Many companies are bought and sold on the basis of the knowledge they contain. On balance sheets, this is shown as 'goodwill' values, but in CRM terms it is an asset of tangible value – the names, addresses and all transactional and promotional information for all customers. The long-term value of customers does not appear on balance sheets, but, if it does, it will be an inevitable consequence of a better understanding of CRM.

CRM permeates all levels of strategic planning. At the level of corporate strategy, enhanced customer knowledge means that you can enter new markets with greater degrees of certainty. It can also identify customers under competitive threat and take steps to reinforce their loyalty. At the level of business strategy, CRM provides greater knowledge of particular markets. You can analyse your database to identify specific market and product range opportunities. At the functional level, these same techniques can be used to derive and test product specifications, customer service approaches and promotional options.

PRINCIPLES OF ACQUISITION AND RETENTION

All objectives and strategies in CRM are based on the concept of customer acquisition and retention. However good you are at devising retention programmes to keep existing customers, there will always be attrition or loss of customers. In order to stand still, you need to acquire more customers. This is the purpose of an acquisition programme.

Acquisition v retention

All company sales consist of two groups of customers – new and repeat customers. It is infinitely more cost-effective to retain existing customers than attract new ones. Existing customers have known, identified needs that have been satisfied by your products or services in the past. By focusing your marketing strategy on the profitable segments of your customer base, you will normally produce most of the required revenue and increase your market share without investing in acquiring new customers, which is much more expensive than retention strategies. If retention strategies succeed, the maintenance of customer loyalty has additional benefits. In this book, our focus is clearly on customer retention. 'Loyal' customers not only repurchase, they also advocate products and services to their friends, pay less attention to competitive brands and often buy product/service line extensions.

Customer loyalty is not merely created by cross-selling strategies or customer clubs. To develop effective retention strategies, you need a thorough understanding of your customers' behaviour and needs. Loyalty is a physical and emotional commitment given by customers in exchange for their needs being met. You should view your relationship with customers from their viewpoints. This should help you understand why you are getting your current level of loyalty. As shown in the last chapter, research of your existing customers is a key contributor to planning retention.

Customer satisfaction and retention

Customers are usually seeking:

■ convenience and easy access to the right person in the company, first time;
■ appropriate contact from you and communication from your company;
■ 'special', privileged status as a known customer;
■ recognition of their history with you;
■ effective and fast solutions if and when problems arise;
■ appropriate anticipation of their needs;
■ a professional, friendly two-way dialogue.

Using information on the customer database, there is no reason for a customer loyalty programme to be anything other than finely tuned to meeting customers' relationship needs.

WHAT IS CUSTOMER LOYALTY?

Managing customer loyalty is a critical component of CRM. In many companies, the question 'What can we do to increase customer loyalty?' is a recurring theme at board level. Many large companies have joined the select band of companies with tried and tested schemes, while many others are experimenting. Consumers' exposure to invitations to join this or that club must have reached an all-time high. However, loyalty is not about throwing money into marketing programmes, producing magazines, setting up clubs or introducing cards in the vague hope that loyalty will be generated. Loyalty will develop over time if the parameters for the relationship are planned and implemented correctly.

What, though, is 'loyalty'? It is best defined as a state of mind, a set of attitudes, beliefs, desires and so on. You benefit from customers' loyal behaviour, but this results from their state of mind. Loyalty is also a relative state of mind. It precludes loyalty to some other suppliers, but not all of them, as a customer could be loyal to you *and* more than one other competing supplier.

Here are some examples of the differences between state of mind and behaviour.

Loyal state of mind

■ 'I trust you more than I trust your competitors.'
■ 'I understand you more than I understand your competitors.'
■ 'I feel at home with you more than with your competitors.'
■ 'You understand me better than your competitors.'
■ 'I want to learn more about you, but I don't really want to learn more about your competitors.'
■ 'I want to tell you more about me, but I don't want to tell your competitors.'
■ 'I want to know what you can do for me, but I don't want to know what your competitors can do.'
■ 'I want to buy more from you than from your competitors' or, more strongly, 'I don't want to buy from anybody but you.'
■ 'When I have problems with your products, I know I ought to let you know, but I don't bother with your competitors.'
■ 'I believe that you'll deal with these problems well, but I'm not so sure about your competitors.'
■ 'I believe you treat me as special because I am a good customer of yours.'

Loyal behaviours

■ Buying from you.
■ Buying more from you.
■ Buying exclusively from you.
■ Terminating other supply arrangements.
■ Checking product availability first with you.
■ Asking you for information.
■ Paying attention to your information – in the media, face-to-face contact and so on.
■ Giving you information on their characteristics and needs.
■ Dedicating resources to managing the relationship with you.
■ Joining your club.
■ Telling you they're club members, whenever appropriate.
■ Carrying the symbol (such as a card) of your club with them.
■ Responding more strongly to your incentives, promotions and so on than other groups of customers.
■ Recommending or even publicly advocating you to other potential customers.
■ Notifying you about problems.

■ Notifying you about successes.
■ Paying you in time.
■ Adjusting their buying/usage procedures to fit yours.
■ Reordering from you routinely.

From this and the previous list, a few points stand out. These are discussed below.

No necessary conditions for loyalty

Not one of the attitudes, beliefs or behaviours listed above is, by itself, a necessary condition for loyalty to exist. A loyal state of mind is a composite, as is loyal behaviour. Some of the elements of the composite can be very trivial indeed – to you, that is, but not to your customers.

Here are some examples of apparently disloyal behaviour by loyal customers. A loyal customer, when coming up to a major purchasing decision, may solicit information from competitive suppliers. Reasons for this may include justifying the decision, benchmarking, following formal purchasing processes or developing a stronger negotiating position. The customer may even buy from competitors if you do not have the right product or service. This may be to avoid the risk of dependence or if you have temporary quality problems.

Degrees of loyalty

There are also degrees of loyalty. Some customers are very loyal, some less so. Loyalty is therefore developed by approaches that reinforce and develop a positive state of mind and the associated behaviours. The aim is not to make all customers loyal but, rather, to improve the loyalty of those customers most likely to respond. Some customers are more likely to respond to incentives, some to differentiated service provided only to loyal customers, while some may only respond to a combination of the two.

Information

The exchange of information is one of the keys to loyalty and provides a critical bridge between state of mind and behaviour.

Loyal customers are more likely to give information to you because they trust you and expect you to use it with discretion and to their benefit. They also expect you to be able to access that information during transactions with them. The importance of information technology as the 'corporate memory' of customer information cannot be overstated.

Loyal customers also expect to receive more information from and about you, so 'privileged' communication is an essential element of loyalty programmes.

CUSTOMER SERVICE IMPLICATIONS

Loyal customers often believe they get better service because they are loyal. They feel they are rewarded for their loyalty. This has two implications:

▨ loyalty approaches should seek to differentiate the relationship and service package provided to loyal customers from the normal level;
▨ ways of giving 'special recognition' at the point of customer contact should be used.

CONSEQUENCES OF YOUR CHOICE OF DEFINITION

If the state of mind definition of loyalty is used, the focus of the resulting loyalty approach will be on gaining a special place in the mind of the customer and making the customer feel that their loyalty is being rewarded by a stronger or better relationship with you, made visible, perhaps, in a higher level of service. If the behavioural definition is used, the focus of the resulting loyalty approach will be on incentives that reinforce behaviour patterns. Put simply:

▨ for state of mind, managing loyalty is a constant theme of the company's approach to managing customers;
▨ for behavioural, loyalty management operates by means of one or more schemes to reinforce one or more 'loyal' behaviours.

However, it is not necessary to choose one or the other – the best approaches apply both definitions. Just like all good marketing, any incentives aimed at reinforcing individual loyal behaviours are also used to draw attention to the benefits of the overall relationship. Let us see how this can be achieved in practice.

MANAGING LOYALTY

If the above view of loyalty is accepted, then managing loyalty becomes much more than devising a promotional scheme to reinforce the behaviour and state of mind of customers who buy more. Unless a scheme designed to change behaviour reinforces and adds value to the brand, customers' changed behaviour will only last a little longer than the scheme, except where the scheme is used to encourage trial by new users. The petrol retailers were guilty of this with their voucher schemes. Loyalty schemes, by definition, are not of this kind.

Further, managing loyalty means not only managing behaviour but also managing a state of mind. It means affecting the customers' attitudes to doing business with the supplier in the long term, not merely until the next visit or the next purchase. This means that a properly managed approach to loyalty must make customers want to do more business with the supplier in the long term or, at least, sustain their existing level of business.

STEPS IN A RELATIONSHIP STRATEGY

The aim is to retain the highest percentage of customers possible. The key steps in a retention strategy are to:

■ define loyalty;
■ define objectives;
■ identify customers' needs;
■ develop the approach;
■ implement the ability to meet the needs identified;
■ measure and test.

Adopt the definition of loyalty that makes strategic sense

There are circumstances in which a definition of the state of mind of a loyal customer is not feasible. In some markets, commoditization has taken place and companies and their products can no longer be differentiated, although often this is due to the suppliers' own marketing and service failures. If you are in this position, using incentives to reward specific loyal behaviours may be the only approach that works for you. However, we suggest starting with the state of mind definition – perhaps best paraphrased as the desire to do business with you and not with your competitors.

Define objectives

The need to develop a loyalty approach over and above existing marketing, sales and service approaches should be identified as part of an overall audit of customer management. Such an audit might reveal, for example:

■ competitive attempts to target, very precisely, your best customers;
■ falling repurchasing rates among your best customers;
■ falling levels of 'state of mind' loyalty;
■ increasing rate of customers switching away from your products and services.

Sometimes, the need for a concerted approach to managing loyalty derives from your failure to integrate all elements of the marketing, sales and service mix to focus on customer retention and development. Alternatively, it may arise because you identify the opportunity to achieve higher customer retention performance than the industry standard.

Your objectives for the loyalty approach should be set in quantified terms – otherwise, the approach will be impossible to evaluate, whether by research or business performance. These objectives should always contain some financial component if the loyalty approach is not to be vulnerable to the criticism that it makes your customers feel good but has no effect on profits.

Identify your customers' needs (and their propensities to be loyal)

If you are considering introducing a loyalty approach, you must establish – usually by means of research and/or testing – the following:

■ the groups of customers that are strategically important to you;
■ the propensity of these groups to respond to different marketing, sales and service approaches;
■ how and how much do they respond and, in particular, how their loyalty increases, mentally (as measured by research, perhaps) and behaviourally.

Remember, segmented long-term value analysis may indicate that customers buying small amounts from you regularly contribute a greater profit margin and longer-term value than do those who make single large purchases.

Your customer base is the greatest potential market research tool you have. It can provide market researchers with an excellent sampling frame, which is why the formal research process should be built into marketing contacts, involving, where possible, the use of questionnaires and structured telephone interviews. If executed properly, research will reinforce the brand and values you wish to transmit to customers.

Develop the approach

This involves doing the following.

Finding the best loyalty reinforcers

Identify those aspects of the marketing and service mix that can be deployed most effectively (taking into account the nature of your target customers for the loyalty approach) to reinforce and build loyalty.

There is a tendency to focus first on promotional incentives (discounts, free or low-cost promotional products and services, that sort of thing), but these have the disadvantage of focusing on specific behaviours, as the qualification to receive the incentive is usually fixed in terms of those behaviours. A key area of focus should be the interface with customers. Put simply, how you deal with your customers – in terms of managing their requirements and exchanging information with them – should hold the key to sustaining and building their loyalty.

Finding the most valued reinforcers

Find those elements of the product/service mix that have highest perceived value to your customers, but relatively low costs of provision.

This may seem a strange point, but it is the key to most schemes that work in the long term. Financial directors are not keen on giving away profits. The justification for loyalty schemes is that they reduce marketing costs because:

- less has to be spent on acquiring new customers;
- it costs less to sell more to existing customers – because we already know them and have access to them – that it does to acquire new customers.

Loyalty schemes can also reduce service costs, partly because existing customers have learnt how to work with you – hopefully you have taught them! However, these financial benefits may take some time to emerge. Meanwhile, the costs of the loyalty approach continue to accumulate.

Here are some good examples of elements that can be built up into good loyalty approaches:

- spare network capacity – underbooked flights, weekend and evening phone calls, off-season holidays, day-time/summer electricity and so on;
- services that when provided to loyal customers cost less than those provided on the open market – car rescue schemes provided to customers who have their cars serviced according to the manufacturer's schedule, for example;
- products or services with very high marketing costs that disappear when they are provided as part of a loyalty approach;
- products or services that customers are prepared to part-pay for, such as points plus cash;
- service touches that cost very little to provide but are different from what your competitors are providing and have high perceived value – special information, for example.

Define qualification levels and segments
This involves a detailed analysis of the profile of your best customers. We advise starting with a broad definition of 'best', rather than just, say, the top 20 per cent, because the next 40–50 per cent may offer huge potential. Thorough profiling and tracking of their purchase histories, transactional values and promotional responses and sources is vital here. It also helps identify the potential market size of similar customers for the acquisition programme. This is sometimes referred to as a CRM audit. Many financial institutions, when they have undertaken this activity, have been surprised to learn how many customers and families are multiple purchasers of the products.

You must work out which groups of customers you wish to provide the benefits of your loyalty approach for and what the divisions are between these groups of customers. Conventionally, this is done in terms of how much, overall, they buy from you, but there are many other approaches, such as:

■ how much they buy of a key product or service;
■ how often they buy;
■ the spread of their purchases;
■ their potential future purchases;
■ their actual or potential importance as a recommender of your services;
■ how much you buy from them (for reciprocal approaches);
■ how much information they give you.

It is common to set 'tiered' qualification levels, with increasing loyalty commitment from customers matched by increasing service levels and bonuses from you. This makes sense, provided that customers' movements between tiers are normally upwards. Being downgraded is not a pleasant experience in any context, but particularly disappointing for customers who have been 'nurtured upwards' for a long period. One demotion can destroy a relationship built up over years. For this reason, the 'slow let-down' must be carefully designed, with early warning and proper explanation. Also, in cases of approaches concerning consumers rather than businesses, the chance to maintain a higher level of qualification can be by means of a subscription fee. It is important not to let temporary reductions in purchasing (which may be totally uncorrelated with loyalty) lead to downgrading. For example, a member of a frequent flyer scheme may temporarily fly less overall rather than fly more with another airline. Demotivating them by downgrading them immediately makes little sense.

Deliver the ability to meet customers' needs

'Ability' in this context is defined as the support infrastructure necessary to deliver CRM. It includes all of the elements described in Chapter 13. In some ways, it is the most straightforward part of the process – in the sense that the individual components of the approach are normally a remix or enhancement of existing approaches, using all the well-known tools of marketing and service management. What distinguishes the way they are deployed is the consistency of the approach, which derives from following the above methodology. Integration of all customer contact approaches and the brand mix differentiates customer CRM from other programmes. This consistency and integration should come through in all the key areas, such as:

■ briefing marketing service suppliers – advertising and direct marketing agencies, in-house magazine publishers and so on;
■ definition of customer service;
■ staff training and motivation approaches;
■ adaptation/acquisition of customer-facing information systems;
■ setting pricing and terms of payments;
■ policy and process development;
■ system development.

Of course, the workload involved in all these is significant. However, the point is that if your approach is developed logically, starting with proper strategic evaluation and with the right analysis of customer needs, behaviour and experience, then the follow-through should be relatively straightforward, based on a phased approach. Many schemes run into trouble because they are developed in a hurry, to fix a short-term marketing problem and without regard for the opportunities opened up by a more carefully designed approach.

Measure effectiveness

Loyalty approaches must, in the end, pay by producing better sales and profits than would have been yielded without the approach. The term 'increase' is avoided here, because sometimes loyalty approaches are required to stem declining sales and profitability.

If you apply the approach to all your best customers, you can't answer the question 'What would have happened to these customers without the loyalty approach?' For this reason, given that financial directors will (and, indeed, should) ask whether or not it pays, the opportunity to test the effect of the approach should be taken wherever possible. The best opportunity for this is at the launch of the approach, because it is a contradiction in terms to test a loyalty approach for a short period and then withdraw it. So, consideration should be given to how customers can be divided into relatively 'watertight' compartments and the approach rolled out slowly, being evaluated, modified and improved as it is rolled out.

On a more detailed level, whatever stage of the lifecycle a customer is at, it is always worth having a continued series of tests to establish optimum timing, frequency, the exact formulation of the offer and creative treatments.

RELATIONSHIP PLANNING

To be cost-effective, relationship strategies have to be planned in some detail and can result in quite complicated programmes.

The purpose of relationship strategy is to maximize an individual's profitable value as a customer. We rarely use the term 'lifetime value' these days – 'future value' is a more realistic aspiration. Active customers can usually easily be identified from records of current transactions. The definition of lapsed and inactive customers varies depending on the average frequency of transactions in particular industries. In merchandise mail order, a lapsed, inactive customer might be defined as one who has not ordered for 12 months, an inactive customer as one who has not ordered for 24 months or more. However, for goods with longer reordering cycles, these figures might be much longer. If your product is durable and replacement takes place every ten years or so, your customers might consider themselves as loyal to a company even if they have not bought anything from you for five years. For this reason, companies with long replacement cycles for their products try to sell lower-value items (service, support, parts and so on) on a more regular basis. The main reason for this is to generate revenue, but it also works wonders as a way of keeping in touch with customers.

In general, the longer the known long-term value of a customer – or the known *potential* long-term value of a customer – the more promotional activities can be undertaken during the life of that customer with you. At the beginning of the customer's time with you, 'welcome' activities take place. These are followed by promotions, encouraging the customer to upgrade or buy additional products or services. Finally, as the end of the product's life with the customer approaches (such as the end of a subscription or equipment need to be replaced), renewal activities are initiated. It is worth determining objectives and developing specific programmes for the following retention strategies:

▨ welcome cycle
▨ up-selling
▨ cross-selling
▨ renewal
▨ lapsed customers
▨ inactive customers.

Welcome cycle

This is an opportunity to welcome and reassure customers, build loyalty and gain additional information about customers. It also opens up the opportunity of providing your customers with initial benefits. Whether or not a welcome cycle is appropriate will depend on the length of lifecycle of the customers.

Up-selling

Given a positive reaction to the product/service, a natural next step would be to promote higher-value products/services. In the case of a normal credit card, it could be a privileged gold card, with a car, an upmarket model in the range, in music product terms a boxed set to appeal to a buyer of a single CD/cassette album. The appropriate timing of the offer can be determined by previous customer histories. Often this can be achieved by testing and applying the test results using regression analysis to the customer database, giving each record an individual score (or likelihood to respond).

Cross-selling

This is a conscious strategy to switch your customers across product categories. For a credit card, it could be promoting a home shopping service or wine club. For a car, it could be a second car for the family. For a book, it could be a music collection. In both up- and cross-selling, loyal customers should be given some incentive to remain loyal.

Renewal

The length of the renewal cycle should be tested to achieve the optimum results for the minimum expenditure. Inducements to reward loyal customers for their continued patronage are cost-effective tactics. Often a renewal cycle will mean a number of timed, relevant and personal communications before the date of renewal, on the date of renewal and after the date of renewal. Once the customer has passed the final renewal cycle date, the person becomes lapsed.

Lapsed customers

Reawakening lapsed customers is usually more cost-effective than recruiting totally new customers – unless they have lapsed because of a fundamental problem in the relationship (such as product quality) or because they have passed out of the target market (because they are ageing, for example). There may also be problems with the quality of the information about lapsed customers. However, when data on lapsed customers is available to you, its value can be tested, so the profitability of promotions to lapsed customers does not have to be guessed.

Inactive customers

Here, cost-effectiveness is a more critical issue. These people have not bought or responded to a promotion for longer than lapsed customers. Again, however, the answer is to test and compare the results to the acquisition programme in terms of justifying its cost.

SUMMARY

Retention – achieved by developing the relationship – is more critical than acquisition as it is usually more cost-effective and profitable than acquiring new customers. The communications employed in a retention cycle will vary according to the nature of the business, but upgrading or cross-selling approaches can include selective targeting of products, catalogue marketing, telephone upgrading, customer clubs, questionnaires and customer care lines.

The objective of a relationship programme must be to make it worthwhile for your customers to stay with you, which is why a thorough understanding of customer behaviour is vital. There is often a delicate balance between attempting stronger relationships and irritating your customers. In any relationship programme, all possible contact points with customers must be reviewed, competitive messages must be taken into account, optimal frequency must be tested, customers must receive the right products and be assured of service and quality. The next chapter shows how you should bring all these activities together.

9

Integrating CRM Strategies

CONTACT STRATEGIES AND THE BRAND

It is vital to see customer relationship management not as something that is a stand-alone, a separate programme to be developed and operated independently of other business strategies, but as an integral part of the way you do business. Both a long-term dialogue with customers and the integration of the idea of CRM into branding strategy are critical to the success of the approach.

Integrated marketing via continuous dialogue (the contact strategy)

A good overall marketing plan will normally contain a number of other plans for communicating with customers, each constituting one or more campaigns. A campaign is a period of structured communication. During a campaign, customers receive one or more communications and, hopefully, respond to them. The desired end result – usually more sales – is achieved. After a time, when all expected responses are in, the campaign is closed.

However, your relationship with customers should not just be a series of campaigns, unconnected with each other and interrupted by long periods of silence. You should not just talk to customers when you want to sell them something. This would reduce the chances of your selling to them. It would also ensure that customers are not very satisfied with you.

Your relationship with customers should be a true relationship. In it, you should manage customers to achieve mutual benefit and satisfaction. A campaign, therefore, in this context, is just a tool to focus communication efforts. This includes media advertising, direct marketing, public relations, exhibitions and salesforce visits.

Integrated marketing via the brand

Similarly, the elements of the marketing mix are not separate in their effects, but build on each other. CRM is delivered via combinations of different elements of the mix and implementation procedures.

The marketing mix must be determined according to your target market. In turn, your approach to market targeting and the marketing mix is determined by your marketing objectives and the conclusions you reach after analysis of your market (as described earlier). Your aim is to combine elements of the mix so as to achieve the desired effect in your target market.

DEVELOPING A CONTACT STRATEGY

Your dialogue with customers must be seen as a continuous series of campaigns, always reinforcing brand values and designed to form and develop a relationship. Campaigns aimed at selling particular products and services start with identification or confirmation of customers' needs. They end with a series of contacts that yield profit for you and satisfaction for customers. Every distribution and communications channel plays a key role in this. Each channel used in a campaign should move your customers closer to the purchasing decision. Each should also yield information to help you handle customers better.

What is a contact strategy?

A contact strategy is a particular set of steps taken when handling customers. It starts with the initial contact and goes through to the conclusion of the particular phase in the dialogue, when the customer has either agreed to meet your objective (make a purchase, for example) or decided not to.

Different contact strategies are used to manage customers through to the sale – a letter followed by a telephone call or a telephone call followed by a sales visit, say. Contact strategies are formalized by having well-prepared options to deal with different turns that the dialogue with customers might take to produce:

▨ clearer options for customers – for example, not 'Do you want more information?', but 'May I send you our brochure?' or 'Would you like our salesperson to call?' or 'Would you like to come to our next sales seminar on topic X?';
▨ economies of scale – by having, for example, a standard brochure or sales seminar where a dialogue with several customers can be conducted at once;
▨ control over your next step – if there is a standard brochure or regularly scheduled seminars, for example, the process of informing customers can be handled fairly automatically.

The importance of the response

A contact strategy is not just an outbound 'you contacting the customer' programme. CRM depends on the collection, maintenance and regular use of information about customers. In CRM, the response sought, and sometimes unsolicited, from customers at each stage of the relationship varies. It may be a move to the next stage in the sales cycle. Responses sought at different stages include:

▨ placing an order;
▨ information enabling a respondent to qualify as a prospect;
▨ commitment to an appointment with sales staff;
▨ commitment to attend an exhibition, showroom or a sales seminar;
▨ assurance that a prospect has received all relevant information about a product or service – this enables the salesperson to concentrate on selling;
▨ indication of a favourable disposition to buy;
▨ acknowledgement of receipt and acceptance of messages that deliver branding information or support;

■ allowing an easy channel for a grievance or a minor complaint to be registered that, if left to fester, might result in a lost customer.

Customers benefit from a well-planned sales dialogue with you because:

■ they have the information they need to make decisions;
■ their problems may be solved before they occur;
■ they can make buying decisions with the confidence that they have obtained the right information and developed a good relationship with you, which will ensure that the purchase goes smoothly.

Data quality

CRM requires high-quality information about customers if it is to be effective. This information may have been collated from various databases – sales order entry, customer service, salespeople's files, responses to marketing campaigns and so on. The database must support tracking of contacts with customers and allow campaign modelling. It should contain information (provided by *all* marketing and sales groups) about customers, the types of marketing action taken with them and how they have responded. This is critical in managing relationships with customers proactively. A fully functional customer marketing database also allows marketing staff to assess the effectiveness of previous campaigns and therefore target future campaigns more accurately.

The more your customer database is used – with customer information and dialogue information being fed back into the system – the more accurate the data becomes. The more accurate the data, the more able are your sales and marketing teams to address relevant sales and marketing activities to your customers that fulfil the criteria right time, right offer, right place. If this happens, the more the system will be used ... and so on. This should result in better, more lasting business between you and your customers.

If you use several different distribution channels to manage customers, your marketing database may be fed by a variety of operational systems used by different channels to run their daily activities. However, the feed must be frequent – ideally on-line, but, if not, at least overnight processing. A modular approach to operational systems ensures that marketing needs do not compromise operational integrity.

THE CAMPAIGN PROCESS

The elements of campaign design are usually summarized as:

▓ targeting
▓ timing
▓ the offer
▓ creative.

'Targeting' here means the customers you contact. Even the best-designed campaign will yield bad results if it is aimed at the wrong customers. 'Timing' is when you contact customers. This can reduce customer satisfaction if it ignores customers' buying cycles, such as replacement demand, business expansion or moving, seasonality or personal availability – that is, being free to make or take a call. Targeting and timing, taken together, are 'customer-side' variables. They relate to the ability to identify the market.

The 'offer' is the product or products you are promoting to customers, together with the packaging of the product and incentives to buy. These elements are combined into an overall offering designed to meet customers' needs. Your offer is a critical factor in encouraging customers to buy. Sending the wrong offer can alienate customers.

The 'creative' element is how the offer is expressed – the tele-marketing script or the copy of the letter and brochure. The offer and the creative elements, taken together, are 'supplier-side' variables. They relate to your ability to put together the right package for the market.

Campaigns, in a sense, are temporary phenomena, so they can conflict with the ideology of a permanent approach to CRM. However, if campaigns are blended together carefully, so that they are seen as a continuing process of finding new ways of meeting customers' needs and caring for customers, they can be a powerful addition to the armoury of CRM. The aim is that each target group of customers or market segment should feel that every communication they receive or make is a natural part of a strengthening relationship.

Enquiry management

The ability to respond to customers' needs at the time they are expressed is called *enquiry management*. When customers ask you about a product, their interest in it is usually more than transitory – the interest will not disappear if the response takes time. However, customers may be making similar enquiries of your competitors. If your response is quick and appropriate, you stand a better chance of making the sale than do your competitors.

Fulfilment

The term 'fulfilment', in this context, means the process by which the enquiry is managed to the point where the customer is satisfied with the conclusion. Fulfilment may consist of a number of steps, including sales visits, telephone calls, invitations to a showroom, sales seminar or exhibition or an order for the product. There are many different routes an enquiry can take.

Testing

To get the best response, different approaches are tested. Because CRM techniques allow you to quantify the results of every campaign, testing provides a low-cost way of getting the details of the campaign right and maximizing CRM.

Targeting

The ability to manage your dialogue with customers depends on two kinds of targeting:

■ **market targeting** identifying the kinds of needs that the supplier can satisfy;
■ **individual targeting** selecting individual customers who have these needs.

Good targeting, of either kind, depends on the information on the database being of a high quality and using the right criteria for selecting customers for a campaign. When you use the database to select customers, a target customer profile is defined. This indicates the kind of customer you want to attract with the campaign. It gives criteria to use to select customers from the database. Selection is facilitated by the ability to control the target precisely. Controlling selection criteria enables you to test the responses of different types of customers to different approaches.

Management disciplines

All CRM activities require tightly controlled, systematic measurement and management. CRM is often justified by its accountability – you know whether or not a campaign is cost-effective because all inputs and outputs are measured. You can also use it to match information on marketing performance and customers' needs and levels of satisfaction.

CRM AND THE BRAND

The marketing concept that integrates the mix and makes your relationship with customers more coherent is *branding*. This is defined as the complete set of values that customers derive from your offering. These values are created by the operation of the marketing mix on your customers' perceptions. The problem facing most suppliers is that it is not just the *current* marketing mix that matters. Customers have memories. Successful deployment of a marketing mix over a period of years leads to very strong and positive branding.

A brand is therefore an asset that remains valuable even after investment in creating it has been reduced. A strong brand can survive weak marketing for a period. However, like any asset, a brand has a tendency to depreciate. This tendency is accelerated if a brand is poorly maintained.

Investing in a brand usually requires:

▓ maintaining the value added by the branded product range;
▓ continually reinforcing positive messages about it in promotion and the contact strategy.

Well-maintained brands have a value that can be measured. Owning a brand gives you the opportunity to make more profit. Creating a good brand is one of the most long-term routes to survival and growth. Branding is also one of the most effective barriers to entry by new competitors. It is a psychological barrier in consumers' minds that makes them less willing to try other experiences. This barrier also makes them more willing to pay higher prices. A brand strongly associated with good CRM is an excellent barrier to competition.

Brand values

Branding a product is not a question of developing and emphasizing a particular set of product features. Nor is it created by a particular advertising campaign. It is something that exists in customers' minds. Your aim is to get brand values associated with your brand name. This means that whenever the consumer sees or hears your brand name, these values are recalled. When a brand name is strongly established, this makes it much easier for you to get your promotional messages over and the contact strategy more effective, because your customers respond to the brand with a positive frame of mind and are more receptive to further messages as a result.

BRANDING AND THE RELATIONSHIP EXPERIENCE

Branding is not created solely, or even principally, by promotion. In many markets, the most powerful weapon is the relationship experience itself. In fact, if advertising makes branding claims that are not sustained by the perceptions of the experience, it is usually worse than if the claim had never been made. This is because expectations have then been raised and dashed. For example, a bank ran a TV campaign that made relationship claims that were so contrary to its customers' experiences that the advertising was stopped midway through the campaign! If you want to establish strong branding, you must pay careful attention to every aspect of the relationship. That is why branding and contact strategies have been included in the same chapter in this book.

Determining brand values

The marketing mix sustains the brand's values. You need to:

■ determine what set of values you want your brand to have;
■ find out what set of values you actually have;
■ make plans to change the actual values to the required set.

Finding out what a brand's values are is achieved by doing market research. Usually, customers are given a list of products, services or organizations and asked what statements come to mind in relation to them. They may be prompted in this, choosing from suggested statements, or asked for their own statements. The list of products, services and suppliers will include close competitors, but also related products and services and other companies or products the brand values of which you might want to either emulate or avoid.

You can use the same type of research to establish what sorts of values customers would like to derive from you. You should not ask them straight what they would like to have – this leads to wish lists of nice things that would be impossible to deliver. It is better to ask what values they are experiencing and enjoying with other products, services or suppliers. Reports on actual behaviour and the reasons for their liking it are considered a more reliable guide than statements of desires.

Branding is supported by a variety of other concepts. These are discussed below.

Positioning

This is an important concept for translating desired brand values into actual promotional and packaging concepts. It means how the brand should fit into its competitive market.

In positioning analysis, you should focus on aspects that consumers say are most important to them. The aim is to determine the positioning customers want and move the products towards that. Positioning is closely related to the benefits of the brand – what the customer will get out of buying it.

Brand proposition

In the world of advertising, benefits and values can be translated into the brand proposition. This can simply consist of words that express the values and benefits of the brand most succinctly. They sum up what you want to occur in customers' minds when they see, hear of or buy your brand.

Brand personality

This is a term used to refer to the practice of embodying a brand's values in personal attributes – for example, trustworthy, adventurous. It helps advertising agencies a lot when they are determining how you want a brand to be presented.

Competitive presentation of CRM branding

One of the problems facing relationship marketers is how to present the relationship they deliver in a way that stands out from the competition. Customers are subject to so many influences that it is hard to make a real difference stand out. The best way, of course, is to experience the difference itself, but this assumes that the customer has already bought or experienced the service. It is hard to steer a course between a simplistic claim that is just like ones every other supplier of similar products is making and a complicated claim that lists every feature of care and service, which will confuse customers.

Brand support

This means that the features of the product or service and the ways in which it is promoted support the branding. As has been stressed above, a brand must be supported by both the relationship and how it is promoted.

Dimensions of the relationship that offer branding opportunities

Here are some of the areas that offer branding opportunities:

■ information exchanged during delivery – what type and quality of information is given to the customer and by the customer, which may include facts, advice and other help;

▇ environment(s) within which the relationship is delivered;
▇ the physical distance between customers and staff, separation by barriers;
▇ amount of time dedicated by members of staff to each customer;
▇ the roles and attitudes of each member of staff;
▇ the range of relationship options – frequency and types of contact, typical outcomes and so on (as customers generally like to have a choice, you may need to steer a careful course between the large range of choices that customers would like and the small range that can be provided economically);
▇ degree of control customers have over the relationship;
▇ consistency – whether or not the relationship meets or exceeds the required standard each time the customer is in contact with the supplier (note that an overly enthusiastic member of staff can be as much of a problem as an under-enthusiastic one, as they may create expectations that cannot be fulfilled next time);
▇ letters, telephone calls, sales visits, posters, inserts – that is, all contact media;
▇ timing – how long the contact takes, including waiting time;
▇ cost – how much customers pay and what other costs are entailed;
▇ availability – of whatever customers want;
▇ quality – whether or not the relationship is as promised.

If you are not sure how your brand experience emerges in terms of the above aspects, think about it carefully. There must be a link – all these points are elements of customers' experiences of a brand.

10

Processes and Procedures

WHAT IS A MANAGEMENT PROCESS?

A management process is simply an organized way of going about things. More simply, it is a clear specification of how different tasks are to be performed. The elements and visible signs of a process are described below.

Formalized planning and decision making

Typically, in a large company, there will be a periodic planning cycle (usually yearly). Decisions will be made about what is to be done. The tasks, goals and milestones arising will be formally allocated. Once the plan is in force, then progress against it will be reviewed at predetermined intervals – more often if there are problems!

Information flows

The process for managing operations will be visible in the information flows that take place – between branches and HQ, between different divisions in the HQ and between staff within branches. These information flows include regular and exception reports on a variety of topics. These are likely to include:

▨ enquiries received from customers;
▨ sales material dispatched, such as brochures;
▨ credit referrals/application queries;
▨ orders taken, confirmed and fulfilled;
▨ payments;
▨ levels of credit outstanding;
▨ average price achieved;
▨ additional purchases made by customers;
▨ capacity availability and usage;
▨ use of particular facilities;
▨ supplies/inventory levels;
▨ customer profiles;
▨ staff activity productivity;
▨ profit – by staff group, facility, service type;
▨ sales/communications campaign results.

Each one should include:

▨ a data capture and/or generation point;
▨ an actioning point;
▨ one or more destination points for the data.

All this information will normally flow as a result of form-filling and computerized data entry processes at the data capture and generation point, such as a sales enquiry captured in an inbound telemarketing screen. The actioning point is the person or department where the data is sent for review and action. In our example, this would be the enquiry fulfilment department or agency.

Exception reports will normally be required for problem situations and for one-off events, such as campaigns outside the usual routine and new market research. The destination point includes other people who may be interested in seeing the data, such as the salesperson responsible for the account or marketing for analysis.

Computers reduce the need for form filling and document filing. Staff are thereby allowed to focus more on giving improved service to customers. Indeed, computerization allows staff to give data to customers more quickly than was possible with a paper-based system.

Customer databases can be developed so that different people can have access to, and 'view', selected data in a way that makes sense to them and the way they work. Understanding the flow of data at this macro level will help in the development of the IT strategy for CRM.

People processes

In large companies, achieving target levels on the items being reported above depends on someone being accountable for or owning the achievement of each item. Staff members must also be motivated and managed so that they *do* achieve their targets. For example, if relationship management is an important item, their performance in this respect must be managed properly and then measured. This means motivating your staff members, monitoring their performance and rewarding them for achieving target levels. The reward does not necessarily have to be financial. It may take the form of recognition by management or peers or special benefits. Measurement may be formal – for example by means of customer questionnaires – or informal – the manager's judgement.

Defining tasks by time period

In developing processes for CRM, it helps if tasks are divided by the kind of time horizons they involve, whether these be daily, weekly, monthly, quarterly, yearly or related to a special event.

Daily work is the everyday job of managing individual tasks. Daily work for managers tends to differ from the daily work of non-managerial staff. The work of supervisory staff tends to be a mixture of the two. For management, daily work may include:

■ filling forms and data entry
■ filing
■ diary management
■ back-up provision
■ people management
■ problem-solving
■ meeting management.

At the human level, the focus is on such things as checking that tasks are proceeding properly, managing problems, helping people complete tasks, supporting and giving them a lift and motivation.

For non-management staff, daily work includes:

▦ managing customers;
▦ backing up customer management by, for example, preparation, completing post-contact processing and so on.

The focus here is on individual tasks and balancing time spent between them on a daily basis. As the period of analysis gets longer, management routines start to dominate. Weekly routines tend to relate to issues such as:

▦ staffing rosters;
▦ handling typical weekly workload changes, especially between weekday and weekend;
▦ collating daily results and reporting them.

In capacity-driven businesses, capacity utilization is likely to be reported and acted on each week. Weekly meetings with staff for communication, motivation and performance review are common, particularly in customer-facing work situations. This is because the quality delivered to customers must be properly managed.

Monthly and quarterly routines tend to relate to slightly longer-term activities or projects. These are often seasonal. They include:

▦ putting together plans;
▦ implementing sales and communication campaigns;
▦ briefing agencies;
▦ recruiting, developing, communicating with and motivating staff;
▦ measuring performance against budget.

Annual routines tend to relate to major activities and very important projects. These include:

▦ launching a major new service;
▦ development and implementation of a strategic communications campaign;
▦ production of a business-wide plan.

Also included here are longer-term people activities, such as:

■ appraisal;
■ long-term development;
■ promotion of key staff.

There is a strong tendency in all businesses for shorter-term tasks to dominate and, unless you are disciplined, they squeeze out the longer-term ones. Planning, especially, is often displaced by the demands of the moment. This may result in your dealing very well with the needs of today and neglecting the needs of tomorrow. For example, existing customers may receive close attention, but nothing is done about recruiting customers for tomorrow.

For this reason, larger companies create strong processes for all their main tasks. Each task is broken down into its elements. Then responsibility for each element is assigned to specific people. The assigning is usually covered in great detail – what is to be done, by whom, by when, in what form any results are to be presented, how results are to be measured, who is to supervise and so on.

Defining standards

Once tasks have been properly defined and responsibility for their achievement allocated, it is possible to define the standards that apply to performance of those tasks. This means that tasks must be defined so as to have some measured output.

RUNNING A PROCESS

Some processes can be self-administered. This applies particularly if tasks are simple and routine, and all involved in doing the tasks know exactly:

■ what the tasks are;
■ why they are necessary;
■ the consequences of not doing them.

For example, staff members taking bookings or orders know that they have to make certain kinds of checks on availability and capture certain information on a form. All that staff need to carry out this process successfully is the training, a telephone and the forms. They do not need a checklist or a computer to ensure that they follow the right steps. However, staff handling complaints over the telephone may need to follow a more formal process, given the immense variety of complaints. Such a process, using checklists, might be necessary to protect the legal position of the company.

Self-administered processes also work well if managers concentrate on managing the exceptions. This should be by strong positive reward for successes and for working to the process, and by negative reinforcement for staff not observing agreed processes. However, if tasks are not simple or required only occasionally, if understanding about the need for them is not widespread and other such cases, then a hands-on approach to management may be required. In some cases, a document-intensive process may be used to ensure that people think what they are doing and communicate it to each other. This is the case, for example, for most planning activities.

Making CRM work by instigating processes

If a procedural approach is taken, for it to work, the following conditions must hold.

▦ **Staff understand the process** This means that members of staff should be trained in the process as part of their normal training programme. This ensures that conformity to the process comes naturally and is not seen as an additional burden.

▦ **Roles are allocated clearly** Also staff members must understand them and have the skills, time and resources to do them. So, for example, they need to know what they are accountable for and what they can decide or influence. There are few things more demotivating than being disciplined for not carrying out something that you were never told you had to do or were trained to do.

▦ **The process produces clear benefits for staff** For example, it helps them work better, reduces tension or conflict or gives them clear standards by which to judge their own performance.

■ **Staff members are committed to the process** This must be reinforced by management action, via its involvement in implementing the process, setting clear priorities, administering rewards and sanctions and so on. Appraisals must take into account staff's contributions to the process.

■ **Management knows when members of staff are not carrying out their role** Otherwise, individual reinforcement cannot take place. A good process ensures that the right information is available at the right time and gets to the right people. This means that the process should produce routine reports that indicate who is succeeding and who is not.

■ **The process is designed to support your marketing objectives** Also – just as importantly – it must allow staff to work more effectively to achieve it.

Workload planning

The quality of your CRM operations depends critically on proper work design and workload planning. Jobs are built up from detailed task descriptions that, in turn, are derived from your (possibly re-engineered) CRM process. Staff performing those tasks have been measured and timed. Staff with less routine jobs have completed time diaries, to allow wasted time or tasks that should be reallocated to be identified. Technology has been deployed wherever possible to minimize time not spent managing customers and to maximize effectiveness and efficiency during customer contact.

Front-office and back-office tasks

The split between customer-facing (front-office) and company-facing (back-office) tasks must be considered, and systems designed to support each of these functions so that they can concentrate on the task in hand.

Front-office procedures should be designed with the prime objective of serving customers – cost-effectively. They must have the following qualities.

■ Be able to handle variations in the rates at which your customers arrive for processing. If the tasks do not have to be completed while customers are waiting, then a process is required to extract from them all that is required (information, payment and so on) to enable the processing of their requirements to be achieved quickly. If the tasks must be completed while the customer is waiting, then the design of the processes must also cover how the customers are to be treated while they are waiting.

■ Be inclusive. They must deal with both your company and customers and the interactions between them. They must also *work* from the points of view of both the company and customers.

■ Allow for the different requirements of customers and the different types of customer you have. Types of customers will vary from highly experienced to inexperienced, loyal to 'cherry picking'.

The reason for the distinction between front-office and back-office tasks is that it is in the back office where more complicated processing of cases takes place. Examples of such tasks include the assessment of insurance claims, preparation of quotations, statements and clarifications, reconciliation of data and the like.

In principle, all these can be done in front of your customers. Indeed, many newer companies have all but abolished the back office by using computer systems and processes that enable customer-facing staff to process all but the most complicated transactions themselves. However, if they can be organized in such a way that they become the province of a 'production' environment, they can be carried out more quickly and reliably than if they are dealt with by staff whose attention has to switch between customers and complicated processing. Also, different skills and personalities may be required for the two types of operation. The focus of back-office management should be on cost-effective and accurate processing of cases. The focus of front-office management should be on meeting customers' needs while keeping within cost constraints. Buffers may be required between the two to ensure optimum allocation of effort. These buffers may consist of:

■ orderly queuing arrangements for processing of cases;
■ information systems to ensure rapid availability of data on cases on-line, in such a way as to prevent back-office staff being disturbed;
■ escalation procedures for handling problems.

Where the volume of front-office contact is very high, it can be sorted and centralized into an environment designed to maximize effectiveness, such as a national telephone enquiry service.

Planning and managing tasks

Attention should be paid to the speed and accuracy with which information is transferred and processed. Information flowing up from operations should be processed quickly and problems isolated soon after or even as they occur. Planning processes should be structured so as to fit the culture of the organization. If it is centralized, information and decision requirements and accountabilities should be clearly specified. The processes of communication and decision making should be facilitated by the use of standard formats. Diarying of the time of important staff should be closely controlled and meetings properly managed. Computerized decision support systems should be used to analyze results and project manage any major changes.

This professional approach to day-to-day management is not as common as it should be. The focus is more on immediate results than on improving the ways in which these results are obtained. However, the advent of quality programmes in many companies has brought home the message that it is not possible to make a neat division between how work is carried out and the end result of that work – sales, CRM and so on. For example, if customers are not being handled effectively, then other operating parameters start to deteriorate.

Work design

Quality programmes have also taught the importance of specifying every action required to achieve particular tasks. In some cases, there will be branching out from the main task sequence if, for example, the required service or member of staff is not available. The work must then be designed from the point of view of all those involved in the work situation.

If customers are to be cared for, work design must include them. For example, at the moment of purchase, a customer will typically be either waiting at a counter or on the end of a telephone line. Anyone who has experienced the frustration of waiting while an inexperienced member of staff consults a complicated brochure or an unintelligible computer screen will know what the problems are. The best solution is to simulate the relationship as it is delivered. This will provide all the information needed to optimize the relationship from a customer's point of view. In particular, it is likely to reveal information about how customers see the process.

Work layout

In many organizations, customers are 'processed' in the manufacturing sense of the term – they physically move through the location of the service. Too often, the design of these locations maximizes back-office space, puts barriers between staff and customers or causes customers to wait for a long time in uncomfortable situations. The design of environments in which customers are 'processed' are often tested with staff members at their 'workstations' to see whether or not customers' needs are met.

Information systems

As the need for higher productivity combined with more customer-oriented treatment has intensified, many organizations have looked to computerization to cut this Gordian knot. Once information systems only carried information on capacity availability, prices and customer debiting. Now, they cover customers' histories and requirements, too. This means that customers and services can be matched more quickly, to everyone's benefit.

DEFINING PROCESSES AND PROCEDURES

These terms can be defined in many ways. In this book, a *process* is defined as a structured way of handling a series of connected tasks. For example, the process for handling a customer's complaint may involve a set of defined steps, with different options to follow according to the type of complaint and how the customer reacts to each step. A *procedure* is the detailed actions that should be followed to ensure completion of a task within a process.

Of course, how these terms are used is relative. There may be several layers of process. For example, you may have a planning process within which there are further processes, such as a marketing planning process. A procedure to support a high-level policy might be considered a process when it is seen from the perspective of someone involved in day-to-day operations.

Process analysis

Once a CRM strategy has been determined, one of the first steps in ensuring its implementation is to develop a very clear picture of the current processes and procedures in those parts of your company that affect the quality of CRM and, then, to determine how these need to be changed to improve quality.

The tool used here is *process analysis*. It is nothing more than its name implies – a thorough analysis of all the tasks involved in delivering policy. More detailed analysis can go down to the procedural level.

The first thing that process analysis shows up is how confused the real-life situation is. There may be a corporate view on 'how things are done', but this view is unlikely to be sustained by reality. For example, a process may stipulate that certain steps should be followed. Practice may show that these steps are only followed exceptionally, because of the time pressures on the staff concerned. This will indicate the need either to simplify the process (so there are fewer major tasks), make the procedures for delivering each step in the process simpler (such as collecting less information) or change the objective of the process (from minimizing refunds to maximizing customer loyalty, for example).

CRM-oriented processes

A customer-oriented process is one that has, as its main objective, satisfying customers' needs, with a subsidiary requirement of checking the 'correctness' of the transaction, ensuring that meeting these needs causes minimum disturbance and loss to the organization. An internally oriented process reverses these priorities. As processes are the main means management have for making the organization progress, determining whether or not customers are cared for as a result of implementing these processes is critical. For example, if processes are internally oriented, then staff will continually have to fight against these processes to meet customers' needs, which will hinder their ability to drive the organization forward.

Feasible processes

In some areas of policy, commitment to CRM may be more difficult to translate into feasible processes, given the likely variety of your customers' responses to relationship initiatives. Therefore, procedures must be designed to operate quickly as well as fairly. Problems and customer status must be checked quickly. This is why modern information systems and policies that empower front-line staff are required. Also, 'Plan B' procedures are required. These identify in advance the kinds of problems that are likely to occur less frequently and the options available to staff for dealing with them. Plan B procedures must also be designed to cope, as far as is possible, with the unspecified unexpected! Plan B procedures mean staff do not have to break rules or 'get around the system' to meet customers' requirements. They also save costs, as the optimum ways of meeting customers' needs are worked out in advance.

SYSTEMS

Irrespective of the degree of centralization, two forces are increasing the needs for systems support to CRM. They are:

▓ the need for higher quality in CRM – systems are increasingly being used to marshal company resources (including information) to meet customers' needs;
▓ the need for greater productivity in CRM – where information systems carry out the job of automating work that was done by humans, such as keeping records.

The major developments in information systems of use in CRM are customer information systems – in particular, customer database systems. Many large organizations have invested in systems that enable them to call up, very quickly, details of every customer's relationship with the organization – sales, service calls, promotions received and so on. However, these systems can be very expensive and liable to information overload. Their performance slows down dramatically as they get larger and searches for details of customers then take longer to appear. Thus, the need to prioritize has become paramount.

▧ Information about customers should be automated in strict order of priority, measured by the importance of the customers to the organization. There is little point in having lots of information available about customers with whom the organization is rarely in contact.

▧ Where particular customers are attached to particular locations – for example, they are managed by a particular sales or service office – it may be better to decentralize the information to these locations. The corporate mainframe can keep updated copies of this information for corporate purposes, such as invoicing and analysis.

▧ The same applies to the kind of information that customers are likely to require from the organization. There is little point in having lots of information available of the kind that customers rarely need.

▧ The information supplied by the system to policy makers should allow them to identify customers' needs. It should not be simply a record of a few aspects of the relationship between the organization and its customers.

Additional points to note are that:

▧ systems need to be thoroughly tested for the integrity of their data and of their communications links;

▧ staff operating such systems need to be thoroughly trained before they operate them in front of customers – very few things are more frustrating than confused operators and customers immediately suspect that their transactions will fail or be incorrectly recorded;

▧ data quality is crucial to the integrity and usefulness of systems – this has led to a strong emphasis on the part of systems designers on data capture at the point of contact with customers and at other points and includes everything from sales transactions and engineers' service calls to meter reading, telemarketing calls and handling of complaints.

Information systems and performance measurement

In many cases, information systems provide the data that is used to assess how successful staff have been in meeting customers' needs. For example, together with sales data, information from customer satisfaction questionnaires may be used to calculate a salesperson's bonuses. This carries risks as well as benefits. A significant risk is that, if money depends on it, staff will try to influence what goes on the system and, in the worst case, try to alter it. There is therefore a need for very clear system security.

On a more positive note, information systems can make a major contribution to the clarity and speed with which performance measures are made available. The sooner measures are available, and the more clearly they are presented, the more quickly action can be taken. Also, computer systems can ensure attributability. They can show which members of staff are most and least successful in dealing with customers.

Too often, when such systems are designed, the emphasis in designing reports is on the needs of middle and senior management. From a CRM perspective, the key need is for your staff dealing with customers and first-line management to have a fast, clear reporting system – ideally immediately or at worst at the end of the working day.

In telemarketing – where much of the data is recorded as part of the normal business process – immediate reporting is the norm. The standards of telemarketing can be extended to most areas where there is daily interaction with customers, provided that these requirements are programmed in from the beginning.

PERFORMANCE AND PEOPLE

No matter how good your processes, procedures and systems, in all except the completely automated environment, CRM performance depends on people – the subject of the next chapter.

11

People and Performance

Unless CRM is achieved entirely by automation, it is necessary to find the right people, motivate and train them well, put them in the right situation (organization structure, systems and so on) so that they can manage customers well. Even if the contact with customers is not face to face, but by letter, telephone or via a machine, people still have an important influence. The organizational structure that they work in will have a profound impact on their ability to deliver the kinds of customer relationship policies and processes described in the previous chapter.

EMPOWERING STAFF

Staff members who manage customers are usually capable of much more than they are asked to do. That is why policies that empower your staff to manage customers better work so well. It is also why giving the responsibility for improving quality to those who do the work seems to produce the best results. On the other hand, if your members of staff are not given responsibility commensurate with their ability, their attitudes towards customers may become negative. This will be communicated to your customers – usually unconsciously. It is therefore much better to take an optimistic – even aggressive – view of the role of staff in dealing with customers.

This is not an argument for radical change in the way you ask your staff to manage customers. People seem to rise best to progressive challenges. Asking staff members to find ways to make radical improvements quickly may destabilize them and wreck their confidence. Staff need to learn what works and what does not by experience. They may also need some training to help them.

If this approach is taken, staff can take on more, and more can be taken on with existing staff. The latter is important, as people cost money.

THE COST OF PEOPLE

In most Western economies, people are getting more expensive. Rising productivity leads to rising real rates of pay and, therefore, rising costs of employing people. Added to this, in some countries, difficulties in recruiting are being caused by demographic trends – in particular, a scarcity of younger people. For these reasons, there is strong pressure to automate and reserve people for where they really add value to customer management. These trends have been visible in consumer markets for many years – in supermarkets, for example. However, they have also had a dramatic impact in industrial markets – in such areas as after-sales service (where remote diagnostics and service are becoming increasingly common for advanced technical equipment) and field selling (where telephone prospecting and follow-up are being used to reserve field salespeople for the most difficult tasks, such as gathering sensitive information about customers' needs and behaviour, and closing complicated sales).

In areas of activity where face-to-face management of customers seems to be indispensable, automation has been introduced to shorten the time it takes to process individual cases. This allows staff to spend more time selling and handling difficult problems.

MANAGING, LEADING AND EDUCATING CUSTOMERS

The idea that the job of customer-facing staff is just to process cases is not conducive to CRM.

The term 'processing cases' is used in this book to encourage a focus on the 'production' elements of CRM situations. It also recognizes the fact that many organizations serving customers do not see their customers as customers, but more as cases. Many public-sector bodies – courts, Benefits Agency and tax offices and so on – are, or were, like this. Also, a fundamental condition of CRM is that cases continue to be processed, but to a higher quality and to the greater satisfaction of customers.

Staff members are involved in managing, perhaps leading and sometimes educating customers. This is the very opposite of the *laissez-faire* attitude that would be characterized by the statement 'I'll meet customers' needs when they come to me, but I won't encourage them to come to me, and when they come I won't tell them what else they can do to get better service.'

The opposite, CRM approach has the following characteristics:

■ customers are encouraged to make use of all opportunities to develop better and more profitable relationships with the company;
■ customers are led in that direction during every transaction (particularly if unfamiliarity causes them to hold back);
■ customers are educated about new relationship standards they can benefit from.

This may seem expensive in the short run, but it is vital in the long run, to retain customers.

In all this, it is important to remember that the facilities that enable staff to provide this enhanced level of service may be provided, but unless members of staff are trained and motivated to work with customers in this way, the company will not derive long-term benefit from it.

STAFF ATTITUDES

In circumstances where productivity and quality underlie the organization's policies, staff are being given messages that can conflict. They are being asked to process more customers in the same time, but also develop better relationships with them.

Of course, the systems and processes discussed in the previous chapter provide the solution to this problem – an improved relationship is not inconsistent with less time and cost per customer. With the right systems and processes – and, in particular, clear objectives in handling customers – many companies have shown that automation not only maintains but also improves CRM. Many customers actually want to be more in control of the situation than they have been allowed to in the past. If they are controlling the machine, with staff assistance where necessary, the outcome may be better for them.

SIMPLIFICATION OF THE RELATIONSHIP

To allow your customers to be more in control, the relationship may need to be simplified, so that customers can manage it better while not increasing costs by getting it wrong. This can be achieved by standardizing what can happen in each transaction, modularizing the relationship and guiding customers through each module by giving them clear information.

MANAGING STAFF WHO MANAGE CUSTOMERS

From the above, it should be clear that members of staff who manage customers are a special category of staff. To ensure that they will maximize the CRM opportunity, the following rules should be applied.

▩ When members of staff are being recruited, special emphasis should be placed on their openness and flexibility. People with deeply held views about the status of different types of people or about the roles that they should play, should be avoided.

■ Training programmes should be constructed so that they provide continuous reinforcement concerning the objective of managing customer relationships as well as the techniques employees require to do their jobs better – a single blast of relationship ideas at the beginning is not enough. Training programmes should contain a strong role-play element, covering, in particular, problematical customers.

■ Staff should be managed as you wish to manage customers. Here, the rule is 'do as you wish them to'. Organizations that mishandle their staff find it difficult to deliver high standards of relationship management.

■ Distinguish clearly between the definition of a job on the one hand and the mission, or essence of the job, on the other hand. It is the latter that should guide staff, not the former. If a jobholder has to step outside the formally defined job to perform the mission (managing customers, for example), then this should be encouraged. Management should act as supporters of the mission, not monitors of the job function.

■ Reward staff for excellent customer management, but in ways that are consistent with the culture. In some cases, congratulations and encouragement may be enough. If financial reward is required, do not make the reward exceptional, as good customer management should be routine. Often, visibility within the organization (and to customers) is reward enough in itself. However, it is important to ensure that staff who manage customers receive pay that they consider decent, given the norms of the industry.

■ Where appropriate, help staff create an appearance that is conducive to positive customer attitudes. Provide image wear, or at least set standards of dress. If appearance is important and one member of staff 'lets the side down', their attitude may be contagious.

■ Give staff an identity (even a name tag) and a personality, rather than a cipher.

■ Create the front-line management role as leader, helper, coach and motivator, not just as controller. The latter role is by itself not conducive to CRM.

■ Ensure that middle managers do not become isolated from customers. Middle managers – those whose major role is to provide the connection between plans and implementation –

can make or break CRM. If they place too many burdens on customer-facing staff and do not see the consequences in terms of CRM, the result may be very destructive. So, involve them in all training and communications about CRM. Ensure that their role is defined as much in terms of supporting customer-facing staff as those of senior management.

■ Carry out regular audits of staff attitudes, needs and skills, and ensure that they match relationship management requirements. Make sure, too, that they are detailed and specific, as the customer research should be.

INTERNAL MARKETING

Internal marketing is the application of all the disciplines of marketing to external customers to staff. The rationale for this is that many staff are internal customers of the policies and processes of CRM.

Internal marketing follows the usual marketing disciplines of:

■ understanding the market – in this case, what kinds of staff there are, what their needs are, right through to segmentation by factors such as need, attitude and so on;
■ setting objectives – for example in relation to delivery of CRM;
■ creating policies – such as those to help staff deliver CRM effectively;
■ marketing them to staff – using all the required media and communication disciplines;
■ measuring results of marketing, in terms of attitudes and delivered performance;
■ improving plans and implementation next time round.

Many ideas that contribute to your ability to deliver CRM have arisen from this approach. When planning an internal marketing programme, you should find the following checklist useful:

■ set clear objectives about what to communicate and measure the effects of the communication in terms of these original objectives;

- cost the communication as an important input into the management process, and set the cost against the measured benefits (to staff and customers);
- identify the differences between the languages of internal and external customers and match or merge them;
- segment the internal audience according to the types of tasks they are required to do and the benefits they derive from doing them, so that the right messages can be sent to the right people (targeting);
- carry out regular staff surveys to measure the effects of internal marketing – not just to hear the good or bad news about attitudes;
- use a greater variety of media to get messages over – from print, video and multimedia to team briefings (the equivalent of face-to-face contact) and match the media to the complexity of the message, type of audience and volume of people to 'inform';
- use professional communications agencies, if the budget can stand it;
- recognize the importance of creative concepts compared to pedestrian instructions;
- control the frequency and reach of internal communications, so that the right communications are sent out to the right people at the right time – otherwise, there is a severe risk of drowning staff in information and exhortations;
- recognize the importance of mobilizing all staff – wherever they work, as they nearly all have an influence on CRM.

MEASURING PERFORMANCE

Performance measurement and staff management are inseparable. If everything is well planned and implemented, the desired customer relationships should be created. However, you must be sure that the effect is as intended – hence the need for monitoring, measurement and control.

ORGANIZATIONAL STRUCTURE

Organizational structure is a complicated issue. It is easy to fall into the trap of assuming that decentralization is somehow a close cousin of CRM. However, this view is superficial. In large companies, at least, many staff apparently quite remote from customers have an influence on the customer relationship. For example, product planners and even technical researchers or scientists can have an influence, for the extent to which they empathize with customers' needs while planning, creating or designing products will determine whether or not they produce products that make it easier for the organization to care for customers. Information system specifiers and designers can have a dramatic influence on an organization's ability to manage customers. They can make it easy or hard for staff dealing directly with customers to access information the organization already holds on customers' needs, or to transmit information 'commanding' the organization to deliver something that meets customers' needs.

Is decentralization inevitable?

Managing customers does not necessarily require decentralized authority. Rather, it requires clarity on the limits of authority at each level and *clear, fast communications* when reference to higher authority is required. It would be nice to say that the optimum situation is complete delegation, but many a good salesperson has bankrupted a business this way! The ideal, therefore, is clear allocation of accountability in job definitions, while maintaining flexibility to meet customers' needs. Of course, provision should also be made for creation of an alternative approach (a Plan B) for the occasional unusual customer request.

In the end, the choice between centralization and decentralization is less likely to be dictated by CRM requirements than by the culture or style of an organization. An organization that has been strongly centralized or decentralized for a number of years is unlikely to be able to switch to the opposite extreme quickly and without cost. The skills required to implement the opposite approach are likely to be scarce.

Which approach is right for you?

This is not easy to answer generally, but there are a few key indicators. From the CRM point of view, centralization tends to work well when:

■ there is a high volume of customers in frequent contact with the supplier;
■ customers have a well-known set of needs and these vary little from customer to customer;
■ the same kinds of transactions or problems tend to recur and are easy to deal with;
■ the importance to the customer of each transaction is relatively low.

This does not imply that in these situations, customer management should always be entirely centralized. It does imply, however, that policies should be laid down centrally and implemented within tight but simple guidelines.

Decentralization works well when:

■ there is a lower volume of customers, in contact with you at greatly varying intervals;
■ customers' needs vary greatly and there is little commonality between the needs of different customers;
■ transactions and problems vary widely in their nature and significance to customers;
■ each transaction is very important to customers.

Functional issues

The second major issue in relation to organizational structure relates not to levels of authority and their location, but to functional issues. Once an organization grows beyond a certain size, it generally needs to create a number of lines of command to deal with the variety of its activities. Use the following checklist to identify which is the main approach taken in your company.

■ **Geographical area** Setting up branches to operate at particular locations or to cover customers in particular areas. This approach is most common where demand is widely distributed and needs to be dealt with at or near the point of demand.
■ **Customer type** Setting up departments to cover particular types of customers, such as large businesses, small businesses

and consumers. This is most common where these different types of customers have greatly differing needs that cannot be handled by the same kinds of people and/or processes.

▧ **Function or discipline** Setting up departments that carry out specific kinds of tasks, such as marketing, finance, production, research and development. This is most common where the function requires specific sets of skills and performance criteria vary greatly from one function to another.

▧ **Activity or product** Setting up departments responsible for part or all of the process of delivering particular products or services to customers. For example, in a motor vehicle company, there is generally one department for commercial vehicles, one for family cars and one for luxury saloons.

In many large organizations one or more of these approaches are usually combined. For example, a large area branch office may be organized by function or customer type within the office. A combination of approaches usually leads to an approximation of the matrix organization's structure. In the branch office example, finance staff might report to the branch general manager, but have a 'dotted line' report to the finance director of the whole organization. The approach may also vary according to the stage in the production process concerned. For example, in a manufacturing company, research and development might be organized by activity or product. Production might be functionally organized – that is, according to the different activities within production, marketing might be organized by customer type, and distribution by area.

The reason these different approaches to organization pose problems for CRM is that responsibility for meeting customers' needs normally cuts across lines of organization. The processes that connect the different departments will often be designed to meet the needs of those departments for smooth operation rather than to meet the needs of customers.

The more complicated your organization, the more likely it is that its processes and procedures will focus on smoothness of operation rather than on a beneficial effect for its final customers. For this reason, process analysis must seek to identify each process that has been defined according to this criterion and revise it to ensure that customers' needs come first.

PERFORMANCE INDICATORS AND TARGETS

If you are to measure the effectiveness of the activities of your staff and CRM policies, you need to set standards and performance targets. The best reason – some would say the only reason – for CRM is that it is an investment that pays off. CRM must be managed using quantitative data on the extent to which it is being achieved and on the benefits arising from it. Although precise measurement may not be possible in every situation, it must be attempted. This is because good management depends on following a simple cycle of plan, implement, monitor, control.

Properly implemented, CRM, productivity and efficiency go hand in hand. Proper implementation requires that *all* aspects of the relationship with customers be included in the scope of CRM projects – not just face-to-face treatment, but systems, procedures, products, the management practices of every function, even strategic plans.

THE FUNDAMENTAL FINANCIAL PREMISE OF CRM

The fundamental financial premise of CRM is that any direct costs of CRM can be set against a variety of benefits. These include:

- higher revenue and profit from increased customer retention and more business with retained customers (higher long-term value) – increasing customer retention can be termed a *revenue defence* benefit;
- revenue from new customers, attracted by the company's reputation (word of mouth, promotions or other means) or resulting from (in business-to-business markets) buyers moving between organizations;
- reduced costs of quality – for example, volume of queries and disaffected customers is reduced;
- reduced costs of complexity, as ways of meeting customers' needs are found that involve less complicated processes and policies;
- reduced direct costs, as customers are allowed to take over those parts of the relationship that they themselves want to do anyway;

■ reduced cost of sales, as more expensive channels of communication with customers are replaced, at least in part, by less expensive channels.

People performance measures, process performance measures, system performance measures and, in fact, any other performance measure should be related, indirectly or directly, to one or more of the benefits on the list above. Measuring against these benefits helps keep a clear focus on why something has been set up.

Such benefits take time to pay off. Strictly speaking, you should carry out a net present value calculation to work out whether or not the action is likely to be worth while. The problem with such evaluations is that they involve forecasting the likely outcomes of the change. Although market research can give some indication of the benefits that will arise, in terms of the likelihood of customers remaining loyal or buying more if practices are changed, such intentions data is notoriously suspect. However, if you are committed to CRM, you will be making changes continually and so should develop a sense of the kind of variations in customer behaviour that are likely to result from changes in policy.

TESTING POLICIES

You can test changes in CRM. If you have branches for dealing with customers, or deal with customers mainly by means of direct marketing techniques (mail, telephone, direct salesforce), you can test an approach on one group of customers. If it works, it can be extended to others. For example, a major airline followed a policy of keeping one group of customers very fully informed of every offer it was promoting, and of a variety of other activities it was engaged in. Another group of customers was given the bare minimum of information. The loyalty and ordering rates of the latter started to fall relative to those of the former. The profit yielded by the additional sales more than outweighed the costs of sending the extra information. In addition, the more informed customers recommended the company more often, so additional benefits might have accrued by word of mouth.

TARGET LEVELS OF PERFORMANCE

It is very difficult to predict the returns to customers, so it is hard to set targets. However, targets based on testing have the dual advantage that they are likely to be more realistic and that staff will perceive them as being feasible and therefore put more effort into surpassing them.

CRM targets are of three basic kinds:

■ **input targets** which measure the work that is input into the CRM process, such as more cases processed to quality standards, reductions in lengths of queues and so on;
■ **output targets** which measure the results of CRM in terms of what customers do – stay loyal, buy more, complain less, say they are more satisfied, write more complimentary letters and so on;
■ **intermediate measures** which relate to what happens to the customer during your processing of their case, such as making contact more frequently to ask for information.

Once these measures have been identified, the relationship between them should be measured.

Setting standards

To ensure that operations are delivering as planned, relationship management standards must be set. These should be based on:

■ **financial targets** these state what must be done for efficiency objectives to be achieved;
■ **relationship delivery targets** as delivered to customers, based on technical measures such as speed of information delivery to customers;
■ **market performance targets** such as share of the market, your share of the customer's budget, rising sales levels – all of which are particularly important in a competitive environment;
■ **customer satisfaction targets** measures of customers' relationship perceptions.

Quantifying standards

You should quantify all these standards. Do not confuse measurement against targets with research. Research is carried out mainly to find out what policies to implement or what problems to address. Measurement is undertaken to assess performance in implementing policies. Of course, the two do not separate cleanly. However, the distinction is important because measurement dressed up as research may be incomplete and bring research into disrepute. The golden rule here is not to decide policies until the situation has been researched, and not to measure until people and systems have been set up to achieve targets and targets have been agreed and communicated.

Although it should go without saying, it is always worth checking that your standards and their associated targets are:

■ **feasible**   in the sense that they relate to areas that members of staff can in practice control by their actions;

■ **credible**   in that staff believe that they can be achieved, that their measurement can be more or less objective and that they really do contribute to the well-being of your organization and its customers;

■ **focused**   on your customers and on the policy areas that are most important;

■ **relevant**   they must cover the major interfaces between you and your customers, as revealed by the contact audit;

■ **reliable**   they must be part of a well-considered and stable policy that endures, so staff members know that if they help achieve them, they will not be told (now or in the future) that their performance was irrelevant;

■ **objective**   in the sense that it should be absolutely clear when and by how much the situation is improving (or deteriorating);

■ **prioritized**   in the sense that staff know which are the most important, as determined by the mission of people's jobs;

■ **clearly beneficial**   to the *supplier* – they must contribute to your mission and objectives – and to *customers* – they must help meet customers' needs;

■ **competitive**   in the sense that they are set bearing in mind competitive offerings, and at least some standards should lead to the creation of a significant difference, to a relationship that has clearly describable advantages over those offered by competitors;

■ **progressive** in the sense that they are not fixed but continue moving forward and changing according to evolving customers' needs;

■ **presentable** they must not be so complicated that staff do not understand what they are or how to achieve them, which leaves plenty of scope for creative presentation.

Try to ensure that most of the data needed for assessing CRM performance arises from the normal information flow rather than from special research. Research is costly and should only be used where its value has been clearly demonstrated. Try to match staff and customers' perceptions and attitudes with financial and market performance. Many CRM problems are picked up first of all in financial figures, then in commercial surveys and traced back to staff attitudes that are the result of poor management processes. This is a long way round and rather expensive. The ideal is to pick a problem up at its point of origin – such as those occurring when there is a change in a process – not when it has affected financial performance.

KEY PERFORMANCE INDICATORS

The number of indicators that can be used to measure attempts to improve relationship management is very great. However, it is easy not to see the wood for trees. So, identify which ones are key performance indicators – those that are so important that achievement of the target is well rewarded, and failure to achieve it a cause for immediate remedial action. These indicators should be chosen so they are closely related to your objectives. You must ensure that they are related to what customers view as the key performance criteria.

Here are some examples of key performance indicators. These can be used for the business as a whole, or for certain parts of it, eg business units, divisions, channels or market segments. It is also advisable to compare company performance with industry performance. Comparisons with different units within companies are also valuable. The most important elements to analyze are as follows.

▓ Number and quality or value of customers – how these are changing, and how they are forecast to change, ie longer-term customer value. This can also be expressed in terms of how many customers of different quality you are losing, keeping, gaining, upgrading or reactivating, and how many customers are changing, eg improving or reducing in value to your business.

▓ Order patterns of customers – how they are changing, eg in recency, frequency, category and value.

▓ Sales contacts, and promotional contacts – the results these give in relation to targeting, contact rates, responses and sales.

▓ Share of business – how different customers can give you more or less of a share of business, and how this is changing.

▓ Additional products and services – the extent to which customers buy these from you.

▓ Customer satisfaction – revealed by the number and content of customer queries and complaints.

▓ Cost to serve (sales, service and support) – absolute and in comparison with revenue.

SETTING TARGETS

CRM must be underpinned by a clear framework of measurement that shows whether or not customers are really being managed well. These measures must be closely related to your overall strategy and provide a basis for setting targets for individuals and groups (staff and customers). These targets should then be adjusted in the light of experience and, ideally, improving performance. Monitoring of performance against these targets should be a prime input into appraisal of staff and their managers and be used to control day-to-day policies.

There are many ways to measure effectiveness. In the end, the most important results are customer satisfaction and brand support and how these are translated into financial measures, such as revenue and profit.

ENSURING CUSTOMERS ARE VALUABLE

Longer-term performance should also be evaluated. This evaluation helps answer the following kinds of questions.

- Should a particular kind of customer be recruited?
- How much should you pay to recruit new customers?
- What methods should be used to recruit customers?
- How much credit should new customers be given?
- What is it worth to the company to reactivate lapsed customers?
- Which customers are profitable now and how profitable are they?

Statistical models are often used to help answer these questions, and much experience of managing customers is built into such models. The more experience you have with your database, the more easily you can develop such a model.

VALUING CUSTOMERS

Customers are expensive to acquire and not easy to keep. If you neglect the acquisition and retention of customers, you will incur high marketing costs relative to any competitors that take more trouble. The marketing information system must therefore give an accurate and up-to-date picture of acquisition and retention. The relevant management report is the *customer inventory*. This shows customer gains and losses, classified in various ways – by type of customer, type of product typically bought and so on.

If acquiring customers is expensive, why do it? Over the period of a customer's relationship with you, the customer may buy many times, across all your product range. The figure arrived at when the customer long-term value equation has been worked out is a measure of the net present value of all future contributions to overhead and profit that customers make. It is hard to calculate, but an approximate answer worked out (to a prescribed formula) quickly is far better (and, in practice, will be almost as accurate!) than a more exact answer calculated as part of a major consultancy project. To value customers, you need to know:

- your customer inventory and your recruitment, retention and *attrition rates*;
- how much customers in various segments are worth to you, on average;

▧ how much it costs to acquire customers of various types;
▧ how much it has cost you to manage the relationship – the cost of marketing, sales, service and sometimes distribution.

If you can compare the figures from before and after the introduction of the CRM concept you can calculate the value of the approach, approximately. The motivation for doing this will probably be a challenge from members of senior management who are not convinced that the approach adds value. They have every right to challenge it where costs are being increased in a business. For this reason, it is always worth taking 'benchmark' figures from your customer database prior to introducing CRM so that the:

▧ benefit can be demonstrated against this benchmark;
▧ costs and benefits of relationship enhancement are kept in a true perspective.

12

CRM Technology – Today and Tomorrow

This chapter focuses on the management aspects of information technology (IT) required to support different types of customer management. It:

▨ identifies the key areas that marketing, service and IT staff should focus on in developing their overall approach to customer management;

▨ summarizes the experiences of the companies we have researched and identifies the key learning points distilled from this experience.

THE HISTORY

In the 1980s, the drive towards the use of IT in marketing and sales was intuitive, rushed and generally poorly focused. There was little understanding of the critical success factors that are at work when different customer management technologies are brought together to function within new management processes. The result has been delays and cost overruns. Symptoms of failure in this area include:

▨ tactical solutions (possibly) meeting today's requirements, but making tomorrow's hard to manage;

▓ poor choice of technology because users' needs were not really understood, so that the resulting system performs poorly – in some cases, not at all;
▓ difficulties in convincing users of the benefits of the technology;
▓ overspend and overspecification, normally because there was no clear focus, so it was decided to try to cover all possible requirements, with the result that few requirements were met fully.

The result is that many projects have not delivered. The most common failure is investment in a large customer database development that has failed completely or ended up as a large 'mailing engine' with no positive impact being experienced at the point where customers are really being managed, such as in the call centre. As a result, outsourcing has become very popular again, because of these internal failures and in order to limit risk and cost. Outsourcing tends to go in phases for this reason, as companies fail to learn from each new wave of technology. However, some companies are starting to learn from this.

One of the principal causes of failure – poor communication and integration between IT and marketing functions – is being remedied in some companies. Their IT and marketing communities are learning new ways of working together. This includes involvement in each other's strategic planning processes and joint training. There is some debate about whether it is the so-called 'legacy systems' that are the problem or failure to consider how systems can be adapted to *improve* performance, as opposed to how systems can be radically redesigned to achieve perfect performance.

Many large companies have been optimistic about the extent to which a single customer database can cope with all the operational, marketing and strategic needs of a business and so have come badly unstuck. Many companies therefore recognize that systems development in this area will be something of a compromise for many years to come. However, most expect to be giving increasing emphasis to the integration of marketing and service applications, with the big database engines behind them increasingly being required to perform as database servers for these applications. This means that they will be able to be optimized for this purpose. In addition, older systems can be effectively 'fronted' and migrated/updated over time. This is often the best way for established businesses to introduce CRM.

For example, a complexity common to most large business-to-business marketers is linking customers together by installation/site/negotiating point level to allow the overall picture to be seen. Transaction systems do not make this easy. Similarly, processing of the vast volumes of retail data is a problem. However, having a clear strategy on separating out the transactional needs from the analytical needs allows a retailer to hold data at different levels for different purposes. This ensures good performance for customers is combined with the detail necessary to allow sophisticated segmentation, though the latter should not be overrated in terms of business benefits. In most sectors, it seems that the early thinking that it was possible to run all aspects of a business on a single database has been replaced by a view that transaction and analysis systems should be separated.

There has been an increased understanding that operational management requires a more integrated approach to systems, such that the different types of systems that hold customer data and related information should be accessible (with varying degrees of ease) by operating functions – sales, service and transaction processing for example. In particular, a full customer management cycle data architecture is required. This means collecting the key data needed to manage the full cycle and using it for planning, decision making, action, measurement and so forth. Data quality is key to the effectiveness of this cycle. You need to ensure that you recognize existing customers when you are recruiting new ones (de-duplication). You must also collect valid data about events. Examples of this include:

■ what campaigns customers responded to;
■ by which channel;
■ what follow-up was requested;
■ what modes of contact individual customers prefer;
■ what the key events (for example, life-stages) are that segment them for targeting, timing, the offer itself and so on.

A SENSE OF PERSPECTIVE

Many of today's most successful customer management technologies were pioneered in the 1980s and before. The pioneer industries were either direct marketers (such as mail order and publishing companies), users of large salesforces (such as suppliers of business equipment) or combined the two (such as a few financial services companies). Some of them managed to change their focus from products to customers. Today, many trends have accentuated the need for deployment of the technologies they pioneered. These trends include deregulation, increased competition, globalization, cost pressures (particularly headcount reductions) forced by economic conditions, channel diversification, customers' desire for service that is personal, low cost and direct, and, of course, the falling price of computing and telecommunications technology. Our experience is that technology is no longer the main constraint – if it ever was. However, data often is, which is why there is an increasing tendency for companies to regard data as an asset, not a cost.

There are still many problems with the processes for using information systems and data. Many processes are slow, expensive and cumbersome. Many organizations are still very 'command and control' oriented – that is, there is a focus more on controlling the impact of customers on the organization than allowing customers to obtain better service from the company. Distribution channels and processes that were stars 20 years ago – the salesforce, branch network and so on – become dogs for the mass-market business or consumer. Still, the culture of operations, rather than customer acquisition and retention, dominates many organizations. At the same time, many new entrants have found that their lives have been made much easier by the 'it'll never work' scepticism of existing suppliers.

In these circumstances, it is not surprising that there is a long trail of casualties. These include:

■ unfinished data warehousing projects;
■ legacy systems nightmares exacerbated by mergers and acquisitions;
■ technology departments running projects because marketing staff lost interest or impetus or simply left;
■ information capture focused on risk avoidance (insurance, complaints), not that required to target good customers;
■ severe skills shortages;
■ lack of investment in interpretative data skills.

It is important to realize that suppliers can actually cause some of these problems. For example, consultants may suggest strategies that cannot be followed through. Hardware or software suppliers with a limited offering may try to gain business by trying to shoe-horn the client's situation into the particular solution offered by the supplier. They will assure the client that their solution will meet acceptance criteria, afterwards leaving it to the client to try to make the solution deliver the required business benefit. Perhaps the two best examples of this are:

■ fully comprehensive data warehouses that cost far more to create than the company is ever likely to earn in business benefit;
■ database analysis packages that are bought and remain unused.

Today, however, a more realistic technological perspective is apparent in some of the companies we researched. There is an acceptance that you never arrive at the chosen destination, but a continuous stream of benefits is gained along the way. Meanwhile, having a map is critical, because it tells you which is the right direction. There are always new challenges – the 'settle down' state is an illusion. Also, investment never stops.

Perhaps the key point to remember about technology is that our work on customer management technology shows a stable approach to the deployment of technology in managing customers works the best (Stone, M et al, 1998, *Relationship Marketing: The technology*, Policy Publications). There needs to be a clear model of customer management (in terms of acquisition, retention and development) and a clear IT model to support this. However, marketing staff are often on the lookout for the next job and the average tenure in a chief information officer position is less than two years in the US. So, it is not surprising to find that while 50 per cent of IT projects fail, 80 per cent of IT projects in sales and marketing fail to meet their objectives.

Stability of approach does not necessarily mean a fixed strategy with a clear end point. Rather, it means a journey in a consistent general direction, but it needs to be made knowing that the speed of progress and precise direction at any one time will depend on a range of factors, such as current business priorities and tactical market opportunities. It is the consistency of general direction that helps companies avoid conflict between, often tactical, actions. One of the main consequences of tactical management of this area that is not strategic is severe failure in data quality and in delivery of data to the point of usage. Often, the last thing to be considered is how the data that will be used to manage customers will be maintained and updated and how its quality will be ensured. Overambitious data collection, maintenance and delivery requirements resulting from unrealistic customer management models lead to poor, expensive performance of customer management systems and poor customer service. The whole question of data strategy and quality is considered in our previous work (Stone, M et al, 1998, *Building Customer-focused Data*, Policy Publications).

One option is what is called a 'layered approach'. This involves bringing the records into what is called a system of records. Then, a distribution database is used to deliver the data to the required functional areas. In this way, the data flows can be understood and the system designed to handle them. Data being accessible at the point of sale is all about the relevant information being delivered to it in a timely and up-to-date manner.

HOW TECHNOLOGY OPENS UP NEW OPPORTUNITIES

Most companies who interface with very large numbers of customers (usually but not always final consumers) are faced with strong competitive pressures and so are looking for ways to maintain the quality and reach of their interface with customers while reducing costs. Customers' expectations continue to rise – they want more, faster, better, cheaper. Whether or not customers ask for it, competitors will provide it, so companies feel under pressure to innovate so most are actively exploring new technologies. However, the very size and scope of their interface with customers means that changing it is expensive, so most are confining themselves to experiments and pilots. However, improvements in customer management achieved via these systems may simply lead to increased costs if technologies are not also used to expand business or reduce the cost of managing customers at different stages of the relationship – recruitment, retention, development and so on.

Great progress has been made in computerization at the customer interface – the point of sale or service. Examples include kiosks and Internet and extranet pages that provide a full shop window in limited space, including all the information enquirers need and instant ability to 'buy', including on-line credit checking. This not only ensures that customers find it easier to be recruited or serviced, but that more customer data is available to suppliers. The problem often lies in a failure to use this data subsequently to achieve higher standards of customer management. This includes recognition of existing customers, which is strongest in telemarketing environments, but generally weak in counter service and similar situations. Of course, in retail environments, this is based mostly on plastic card technology (magnetic strip or smart card). In both environments, the updating of data from different sources (transactions/billing, campaign response, customer service and so on) is still a problem for many companies. Customers also want access to information about offers, their previous and current transactions and the state of their relationship with the supplier. Current examples of this include the demand for remote access for home banking or self-management of investment portfolios.

However, customers' expectations that data about them will be available at all points of contact with them and used constructively is causing much improved customer recognition, customer data availability and associated processes to be built into the new generation of system specifications. Today, though, few customer-contact systems can display a *full* and relevant customer record quickly – that is, so fast that the customer barely notices the delay. Most companies realize the need for improvement here, and many are working on upgrading the information flow to and from these customer-facing systems and helping operators (sometimes customers themselves) navigate their way around. Most companies also realize the continuing need for training their customer-facing staff, for, no matter how much 'expertise' is given to the system, there is a continuing need for the human touch. In fact, it can be argued that using smart systems to liberate operators to become human again is a key to competitive service advantage. For example, the insurance company AIG Landmark does not favour prescriptive telescripts and efforts are made to match appropriately selected and trained staff to different customer groups.

In inbound telemarketing, the area where some of our respondents expect to make most progress is in intelligent inbound systems that manage the script according to customers' responses and use information already held on the database. Most companies expect their use of computer telephony integration will increase rapidly over the next few years with information exchange and customer recognition becoming more common. This will lead to much enhanced segmentation strategies for customer management, calling being triggered by segments' needs. Also, the triggering of calls by key events is likely to increase – for example, what we call 'intensive care' calls triggered by service problems or changing decision-making units. In the business-to-business market and some consumer markets, call centre/field sales teamwork will also become key, as it often is in service and technical support environments. This will apply even in mixed or hybrid channel marketing, in which a company addresses a given set of customers via a variety of channels that may apparently conflict with each other but actually meet different sets of needs.

At the same time, many companies will continue to make the error of thinking that advanced telephony is a substitute for strategic thinking. An advanced call centre working to the wrong brief is like a powerful army marching very fast in the wrong direction!

However, many companies have found that using a customer database as part of a process to improve service has been an important justification for investment. Doing the simple things right – writing to or calling the right customers, getting their details right at the point and moment of contact, then following up by handling customers quickly, efficiently and professionally – seems to be the key here. However, there is a strong tendency to overcomplicate the matter – from both systems and process perspectives. This leads to what we would regard as overspecified systems and processes that take too long to deliver or may even never be delivered. Here, the key is to view things from customers' perspectives and avoid investing in approaches that make no significant difference to the way customers are handled.

One way in which companies try to overcomplicate their decision-making processes in this area is by trying to impose a spurious rationality on the process by which customers are managed. The commonest form of this is trying to allocate different customer types to different distribution channels or different communications media. Today, it is clear that customers are happy to be managed and manage their suppliers using a variety of distribution and communication channels. In the new world of 'hybrid marketing', it is accepted that new technologies and channels can be used in a complementary rather than competitive manner, to reduce costs and recruit, develop and retain customers more effectively. For example, it needs to be understood that e-commerce is often very effective in combination with other methods of communication in managing existing customers, but sometimes less effective in customer recruitment, where the call centre can be very strong. Unless this more flexible approach is taken, too often new technologies such as call centres and e-commerce can add costs and create conflict rather than benefits.

ACROSS-THE-BOARD IMPROVEMENTS OR 'TOP VANILLA'

The literature of database and CRM is replete with phrases such as 'total customization', 'market segment of one' and similar (see Flint, D, 1996, 'Sharpening the customer focus', IT Management Programme). However, in our research, we have encountered increasing numbers of marketing directors who are becoming deeply frustrated by the large gap they perceive to exist between their reality and these fine theories of customer attunement. The latter are often supported by disparate examples, but there are very few documented cases of a company achieving it across the board. For example, BT and MCI achieve a high degree of customer attunement in their consumer mailing programmes, but find it harder to deliver this in their call centres. Worse, they have seen, and often suffered the impact of, new competitors coming in and offering a very high level of undifferentiated service, using tried-and-tested IT, such as the 'new breed directs'.

HIGHLIGHTS OF CHANGE

IT and the marketing, sales and service approaches that it makes possible hold the key to the future of CRM – particularly in its transparent guise. However, what has been the experience so far? In general, it can be summed up as steady improvement in mass markets, with the occasional dramatic leap forward. In the emerging electronic fortress and, more generally, in business-to-business markets, the pace of progress has been more impressive. The highlights are described below.

THE OLDEST TECHNOLOGY – DIRECT MAIL

A vast volume of customer communication is still carried by mail, and in Europe the volumes are still increasing, in contrast to the US where levels are much higher but declining. Where the postal authorities have worked closely with the direct marketing industry and designed products and services to meet its needs, the rise in volume has been the healthiest and most sustainable. However, even here there is still room for improvement – on both supply and demand sides. Electronic services (such as the downloading of data to local postal distribution centres to print for high-volume local delivery) still show room for improvement. However, most important of all, marketing management needs to understand the potential for these new services and build them into their media plans.

Poor targeting has led to some criticism of database marketing and mail distribution. However, most companies we have researched are working hard to improve their targeting. In many cases, the problem is that the extension of the direct marketing approach into new areas seems to be running ahead of companies' technical capabilities (typically customer databases and their applications). These companies do not have the time to develop more tightly targeted customer recruitment and retention activities. In particular, the use of mailings in customer retention and development is understood by relatively few companies (American Express, Barclaycard, BT, British Airways, for example), though others are catching up fast (such as retailers and a small minority of financial services providers).

More recently, many companies are racing to implement a direct mailing capability, but without full consideration being given to the quality of data required and without researching and clearly defining the customer proposition and follow-through. Most companies have discovered that responses to targeted mailings can improve substantially, particularly following datamining exercises that identify highest response/value segments. However, it should be noted that clarity of offer and relationship strategy and brand strength are just as important in ensuring response levels. In this respect, the basic truths of marketing still apply!

TELEPHONY

Call centres

Anywhere advanced call centres (advanced integration of computing and telecommunications to handle calls to and from customers) can be used, the progress has been fast. The best examples of this are home shopping channels and the new wave of direct service providers such as financial services, travel and leisure, where the lack of the need to deliver anything but documentation helps! In some cases, simply publishing a helpline number and managing the calls properly has dramatically increased the openness of companies to their customers. This practice is becoming standard in packaged consumer goods.

Voice/data transfer and sophisticated voice recognition systems (operatorless) are becoming more important as consumers become more educated about this way of doing business. However, telemarketing still has a long way to go – not in theory terms, as most companies know what it can do, nor in technology terms, because what it can do is way ahead of what we want to do, but in practice terms. Most companies are still learning how to manage it and integrate it with the rest of customer management. Inbound telemarketing needs intensive work, particularly as the focus moves from cost containment to value management. However, managing customers according to their current or expected future value is still so poorly done by many companies that it is hard for inbound telemarketing to perform. The key question that the inbound telemarketer needs answered is 'Is this customer valuable?' In most cases, companies have not worked out the answer.

Using profitability scores and simple 'traffic light'-type signals to operators to show which actions would make a customer more valuable is another angle that is being explored by a number of companies, including American Express. For example, payment by direct debit might be suggested or customers might be offered an upgrade or increased line of credit. Here the emphasis is not just on recognizing customer value but also on trying to increase it. There is, of course, the more usual type of 'valuable customer' recognition – by product type. For example, American Express Platinum cardholders are, by their very nature, valuable customers. However, in this market, the proliferation of gold- or silver-coloured cards with low entry levels by mass issuers has diluted some companies' ability to use this as a means of recognizing valuable customers. The same applies to the general offer of 'personalization' – 'your very own ...'.

In business-to-business markets, the use of clear categories of account management (such as key accounts) has resulted in the introduction of simple customer-type flags or product recognition codes. These trigger a particular type of response from the call centre operator. For example, in a field service operation, a customer might receive a two-hour as opposed to a four-hour response time when they call for an engineer.

Our experience of call centre implementation is that many of them are designed from the company out to the customer, rather than the other way round – which is how it should be done. This is because many call centres are put in place to meet one or two overriding company objectives, such as reducing contact costs, gathering more information cost-effectively. Often, a call centre is a location where many customer-facing systems meet in an uncoordinated fashion. Operators of such systems still have to work across many systems, mostly without a graphical user interface. In such circumstances, customers are often asked to wait while the operator hot-keys or logs on to another system to access a different service. For this reason, large companies often give customers the impression that the left hand does not know what the right hand is doing, simply because the operator cannot log on to another system instantly.

The magic telephone

The industry has spent the last few years educating its customers about magic telephones. They can do anything – customers can buy from them, get their queries answered by them, complain using them, file claims on them – and it doesn't matter what colour the phone is. One result is that, more than ever, customers want to contact companies. They want to talk to them for all sorts of reasons – to complain, request information, ask queries, pay compliments, and even buy things. The more loyal customers are, the more they need the company's products and services and the more they want to contact them. When these customers do so, the more important are the things they want to say, the questions they want to ask and, of course, the complaints they want to make! However, customers do not only want to contact their suppliers more. Better customers – the ones companies are usually already in contact with quite often – want to start managing their relationship with the supplier. The old idea of companies 'doing things to customers' and them responding when companies want, where companies want and how companies want is changing.

Increasingly, customers expect to contact companies when, where and how they want, to order products and services in ways they configure. They want to know what options are available and how to put them together. They also expect that when they are talking to a company it will behave as one company, so that if they talk to administration one minute and to sales the next, sales will know about the query they posed to administration.

This is why many companies are thinking about service or relationship centres rather than call centres, as they need a central place in which customer communication can be handled in an integrated manner. We expect that most call centres will evolve in this direction, except in markets where contact with individual customers is infrequent. Part of this move will be the development of a more sophisticated approach to outbound telemarketing, in which customers' willingness to accept calls is better understood, as will be their preferences for the timing, duration and content of calls.

From unsolicited communication to customer-controlled contact

Companies used to worry about complaints, customer feedback or more broadly 'unsolicited communication'. This term was used to distinguish it from the communication that came back from customers as a result of companies contacting them, usually as a result of a marketing or sales campaign. Now, companies have to accept that they must make themselves – the brand, products, services, people – available to customers by an increasing variety of routes. We are moving into a world of 'customer-controlled contact' – at least, that's what some customers want to believe. In this world, the vital importance of managing the initial contact – the moment of truth – is taken as a given. However, for customers, the moment of truth is neither the beginning nor end but often a brief episode in their service relationship. So, companies must not only handle these brief episodes well, but also ensure that they have the right systems and processes for handling the entire relationship.

Understanding the telephone

Most companies now understand when and where the telephone can be used and for which kinds of customers. They can also draw on a range of suppliers to show them how – to design and install telecommunications and computer systems and develop and implement marketing campaigns. If they want to contract out this work, companies can turn to one of the many high-quality tele-marketing services, which can handle virtually any aspect of customer management using the telephone and integrate this with other service and marketing activities. In the last few years, many companies have invested in upgrading their telecommunications systems to improve their inbound call handling. Customer care lines and helplines abound and call centre providers have found it hard to cope with demand. Can they manage the telephone consistently?

There are signs that much of this high-cost investment – in technology, recruiting and training staff and advertising contact numbers – is wasted. Media agency CIA Medianetwork last year published research that suggested that as much as £99 million in direct response TV advertising is wasted annually because advertisers fail to understand the principles of using the telephone as an effective customer contact mechanism. This research project supports Medianetwork's findings. One of our research respondents, Tony Coad, Business Development Director of *The Daily Telegraph* and a well-known figure in direct marketing, set up a project in which financial services companies that had advertised in *The Daily Telegraph* were telephoned. The aim was to see how they handled an inbound call responding to advertising. The process was followed through to the bitter end. Tony concluded that, if inbound calls – and the follow-up process – are handled as badly as the results suggested, either the productivity of the advertising and sales process was being diluted or, if productivity was good despite poor practice, that profit was being sacrificed.

One reason for these failures is that senior management simply does not understand what goes on in call centres and the consequences of getting it wrong. We believe that, until more managers with a strong pedigree of managing in a customer information-intense environment actually run companies, 'customer information-based marketers' will always be frustrated by senior managers who either do not want to know or, worse, attend one guru seminar on 'one-to-one marketing' and return thinking they are experts and drive totally inappropriate strategies!

Consider this. At the user group of one of the top call centre systems suppliers, the attendees came from the *Who's Who* of direct marketing and included many insurers. The attendees were asked how many of them believed their top management teams understood what went on in a call centre and the role of the call centre in managing customers. Less than 1 per cent answered positively. No wonder, then, that the practice is so far removed from the theory. One of the reasons for this is the substitution of a purchasing decision (buying a call centre) for a management decision (deciding how to manage customers via the telephone and how to integrate telephone-based management with other media and the work of sales staff). For the telephone to work well as a CRM tool, the link with the customer database is key – all too often this is lacking. This point also applies in relation to most other customer-facing marketing technologies.

Consistency and thoroughness

Consistency is a distinguishing feature of good contact handlers. Flavours of the month are banished and the key performance indicators of contact management are understood and managed well over the years. A commitment to continuous improvement is evident, as is the avoidance of unrealistic targets. Communication peaks (often as complaints) when new products are introduced. However, the key is satisfaction with contact that resolves the issues, not absence of contact. The best companies tend to collect all the key data and get it to the centre, where it is discussed by managers who understand what the figures mean. Others collect less data and tend to only centralize data on those issues that require centralized or escalated solutions. The rest is lost at local level.

Even if all the key data is collated and analysed, too often this is where it ends. Management does not take action, which results in obvious changes in the field – in how customers are managed – demonstrating the value of collecting the data to actually use.

Difficult questions

Increasingly, companies that rely on the telephone for much of their customer-handling processes are starting to ask difficult questions.

■ What happens to customers when they call?
■ How well are customer calls being handled?
■ What are the effects, in terms of customer satisfaction, increased or retained business, referrals and the like?
■ What stories do call centre statistics hide?

It is this last question that is the most challenging. Of course, companies should always aim to measure their customer management successes and failures by means of the information generated by the systems they use to manage customers. However, there is a limit to this process because they cannot simulate the actual *experience* of the transaction, nor the relationship from the *customer's* viewpoint. While companies can tape calls to monitor how well management thinks staff are working, this does not measure how well customers think staff are working and therefore how well customers think of the company overall. For this reason, companies that are serious about using the telephone in managing their customer relationships are now setting up external monitoring. Mystery shopping of call centres is now more developed, with contacts to verify real customer management sequences, sometimes even using real customers.

One point to watch, with the increasing use of a variety of voice response approaches, is that long voice response introductions tend to infuriate customers, who will often abandon a call or default to human operators in a fit of pique.

THE ELECTRONIC PURSE

This has made a slow start as most consumers are reluctant to desert their current portfolio of cash and cards. However, it is still early days. This said a specific electronic purse – for storing credits for particular applications – is usually quickly accepted. Examples include vending machines, public telephones, public transport and photocopying. This idea is proving particularly popular with closed user groups, such as employees of particular companies and students at particular universities. Perhaps we are being too optimistic in expecting a very rapid diffusion of a technology that, after all, replaces one of the oldest systems still around in marketing – cash, particularly when a competitor, the debit card, has made such rapid strides in the market.

Despite these reservations, the cashless card is now starting to accelerate. Kmart has launched an automated retail cash card that can be used as an electronic gift certificate, cash replacement for merchandise returns, a calling card, budgeting tool for consumers and for promotional programme management. In The Netherlands, most banks are involved in the electronic purse project, known as Chipknip. This covers loyalty, ticketing, identification, public transport and other payments. In Singapore, there is already a basic cash card that can be reloaded at ATMs and used for the purposes of retail purchases, public transport, payphone calls and electronic tolls.

THE CD ROM

This has proved a very viable medium – particularly as a substitute for expensive brochures, such as for cars, and especially when used in direct marketing, where its lightness compared to high-quality paper is a big advantage. Vauxhall is a pioneer in this area. Obviously, any product that needs to be seen moving in order to appreciate it is a good candidate for this treatment. Also, once the material has been digitized, it can be used in a variety of applications.

CD ROMs are now also used to assist staff, by providing very rapid access to complicated data (such as is needed in call centres) and allowing them to configure options for clients (in selling insurance, for example). A particular advantage is its ability to inject consistency into the sales process, by standardizing how complicated products are described. For example, pharmaceutical companies use it to help their representatives sell to doctors, using animation of how the drug works. BP in Germany use invoice and statement data stored on CD ROMs at the point of call with a customer so that even complicated and historical queries can be handled quickly and professionally. Not only does this impress customers, it saves administrative time by removing the need to search files manually and call customers back to revisit the problem with the new information to hand.

One of the limitations of the CD ROM is that, by itself, it does not allow the company to analyse what the customer is interested in, which, of course, the Internet can. However, the two acting in combination can be very powerful. For example, a CD ROM can be used to send customers some of the software required to liaise with a particular company on the Internet, plus a whole variety of relevant images, questionnaires and the like. The CD ROM can then create files on the customer's computer, for updating and retransmitting to the company.

EDI AND E-MAIL, THE INTERNET, EXTRANET AND INTRANET

In business-to-business marketing, EDI's cost savings and improved accuracy continue to yield benefits. It is spreading beyond products and services and beyond order taking/receiving for essential items in the value chain to ones that are 'overheads' – such as office supplies (where the possibility of placing standard regular orders can be a great attraction) – to provision of technical and customer information. Its application is cascading from communications between larger businesses down to smaller businesses as costs fall and more smaller businesses see the cost–benefit ratios changing. Good examples of this include car dealers (especially for vehicle and parts ordering and for inventory management) and, indeed, any other business where the prime route to market is a 'managed channel', such as a franchise, where the small businesses' customers adopt the supplier's systems, too.

The Internet and commercial use of the World Wide Web infrastructure has become much more than an opportunity for organizations with technical products or services alone to set up an interface with customers. Many companies initiated their presence on the Internet with information pages about their organization and products and/or services they offered. The first step to interactivity was the response button creating an e-mail query or comment.

A key feature of the Internet is that, via browser technology, it can provide easy access to the customer management data we have put much effort into creating – maximizing value to the company itself and to business partners and other members of the value chain.

The frequency of access and the nature and number of sales that result often surprise companies that have begun to offer interaction and order-taking facilities. The *nature* of the sales is important, because it shows how far the prescriptive model of CRM could have led to a company excluding customers from its target market.

In some cases, the Internet is providing a dramatic market extension – such as is the case with access to the Relais de France pages from North America. In other cases, such as for retailers, it is providing interesting insights into the way that their customers may want to shop in the future (see Lord, R, 1997, Why go to Tesco when Tesco will come to you?, *Revolution*, 1 (1), pp 48-50, Keogh, G, 1997, Off your trolley, *Go*, CompuServe magazine, issue 3, p 10, and Robertson, C, 1997, Shopping the next millennium way, *Computing*, p 20). However, many of the most significant Internet projects in marketing companies are intranets, or intra-company Internets, which are simply designed to keep staff well informed in an otherwise chaotic marketing environment (see Stammers, T, 1997, Unilever backs intranets, *Computing*, p 2, and Gabriel, C, 1997, Intranets take on new applications, *Computing*, p 18).

Until recently, most large companies have not integrated their Internet activities with their core commercial processes, such as quotations, order taking, direct marketing, customer service and so on. However, some expect to integrate and eventually re-engineer their processes around it, if their experiments deliver the quantity and quality of customer interaction they desire. Most large organizations now have a presence on the Internet. At first, many companies analysed the numbers of visits to sites and pages, in some instances where they were coming in from (which machine). Today, targeted data capture is becoming much more the norm and, as a result, where the access volumes are high, companies already use datamining to analyse who is accessing their site, when and why. Interestingly, the involvement of marketing staff in determining the nature and scope of Internet activities seems to be very high (see Dye, P, 1997, Marketers take reins from IT, *Revolution*, 1 (1), pp 4–5).

The most important change for companies actively taking part in the Internet revolution has been the realization that the opportunities and contexts for building and generating relationships with groups of customers or individuals can be much greater. When considering the target market in the virtual global world, they have to think in much wider terms about the contexts in which their customer base or potential customer base may think of or need them. For a household insurer, getting linked up with those selling houses or household products is key to creating the event opportunity, for example.

More importantly, when they have managed to position themselves well and at the right time, the speed required to respond to queries is much faster than with other media – why? Because competitors will be just a click away! The skills required for Internet marketing, therefore, are also quite different from those used in traditional contexts and are beginning to evolve as a result of testing.

Some companies have successfully started forums for their customers – attracting customers to come and find out answers to questions or interact with one another. IT companies have managed this best to date, as they have the skills to handle the responses, but it is a very good way of finding out more about your customers' views on your product or service and the types of customers you have.

However, the Internet is a new medium, with restricted but rapidly growing coverage. What makes it different from previous media innovations, such as commercial television, is its relatively low entry cost, which means there is a high percentage of virtual junk. Despite poor network support (slow speeds) and unstructured information in the main, it is often used to provide product and service information. Low-cost, high-speed access will transform usage, it becoming a normal information and transaction medium. However, there is little evidence that the underlying installed-base S-curve will be different from, for example, telephone, TV, ITV, video, cable, except that it will move much more quickly. Most users will use it mainly to get information, but an increasing number will use it for transactions, these being made with greater and greater frequency. This usage will be improved by variety in modes of access – it is already available via personal organizers and on some airlines in the USA.

Security of transactions – once seen as the greatest barrier to uptake – is also being improved. Encryption and encoding processes, as well as innovative ideas from companies such as Digicash for linking with smart cards, have even interested the banking and credit card communities.

Home shopping continues to provide an interesting area for experimentation – for example, Tesco Direct and the Tesco Mother and Baby telesales operation. The DIY chain B&Q, which has 280 stores, now has a Web site with 500 pages, including a store directory, outlet details, location map, product listings, project step-by-step guides and being able to order gift vouchers. IBM has an interesting home shopping experiment with Somerfield at its Hursley research centre, where 2500 staff can order and get same-day delivery if orders are placed before noon. There is a £2 order cost and a minimum order value of £15.

One driver of the use of the Internet is higher education, where today virtually all students are expected to be able to access it for research purposes (see Rosen, N, 1997, Students switch from MTV to the Internet, *Revolution*, 1 (1), pp 6–7). However, good marketing technologies are the ones that help us to either recruit new high-value customers or manage and retain existing high-value customers cost-effectively. So, the best model may be the closed user group – one we know, that we manage and manages us using the Internet (very much the intranet model).

Web technology is enabling other forms of relationship management for organizations. The intranet is enabling some organizations to transfer important customer information and customer-related product information to and from those dealing with them in a very user-friendly manner – and fast. The simplest example is the company contact and telephone list, ensuring that customers are not passed from person to person in an organization.

A related idea is to link together a remote closed user group, such as other members of the value chain, in what is now called an extranet. Insurance companies are looking at this technology to support interactions with leading brokers, for example. This cuts out costs for the company and time lost for customers. Some organizations have tested internal process support on intranets before extending them to the Internet as added-value services. The extranet group may or may not be given a highly secure gateway into the company's host e-mail system.

The advantage of this option is the speed with which it can be set up and the limited impact it has on the host systems as links to these systems are now easier to implement. Intranets provide easy connections to the outside world, better accommodate multiple competing suppliers and carry lower acquisition and operating costs than private e-mail or file management systems. These advantages, combined with videoconferencing via PCs, will change the nature of supplier–customer relationships, especially where a product or service can be digitized, such as reports, information, artwork and computer games. The physical distance between suppliers and customers will become even less important to the relationship than is already the case today.

The more generally the Internet and its associated technologies are used in marketing and customer management, the more urgent it becomes for companies to apply the key tools of customer management in deploying the Internet if they are to compete and achieve strategic advantages over their competitors. Here are a few tips in this area.

- The prime reason for using these technologies is to improve value to customers – that is, to meet their wants and needs. Focus on customer benefits is therefore essential.
- Create a vision for longer-term development, introducing additional sites or deepening initial sites, to support your marketing and services and, of course, your customers' needs.
- In many cases, these technologies not only allow you to meet customers' needs better, but also reduce costs of other means of communication, such as looking up details in timetables,

confirming booking (perhaps best demonstrated by their use in booking cinema seats). This is one of the major pay-offs of the hybrid marketing approach.

◾ Harmonize the approach fully within traditional advertising and communication programmes. Ensure that the message and brand are delivered consistently across all media.

◾ Use Web functionality to enhance involvement with the brand, in ways that match the brand. For example, use it to put a human face on the brand.

◾ Use the technology to allow customers to find out the full range of what you offer and do – product, research, product development, loyalty programmes, promotions and so on.

◾ Leverage the facility this technology gives you to allow customers to take control and give you information or update it – by customization, use of push technology and so on – at their convenience.

◾ Anticipate viewers' constraints – whether or not they are able to access you quickly and conveniently, for example. Don't use advanced graphics all the time as this can simply waste customers' time.

◾ Drive traffic – don't wait for visitors to find you, use on-line advertising, PR on- and off-line, traditional ads, backed up by aggressive linkages and cross-promotions.

◾ Keep your offering up to date, topical and relevant to maintain interest, but ensure that it follows a consistent pattern for your loyal audience.

◾ Use the best security and guard your customers' privacy.

◾ Resource and maintain your site adequately.

◾ Measure everything – traffic volumes and patterns, user profile, satisfaction – ideally by means of independent auditing.

KIOSKS OR BOOTHS

These are being experimented with extensively – particularly in financial services and retailing, but also in telecommunications (1997, BT interactive kiosks hit the mark, *Revolution*, 1 (1), p 5). Effectively, these allow customers to select, view, learn about and order products and services, view corporate communications and take part in promotions and order products. They are being made available in stand-alone sites or on company premises. Here, the experience is that there must be a sound business proposition. Many early experiments were technology-driven. Experimenters found that what they were trying to do was actually easier at the conventional point of sale. However, IT and marketing departments are working closely together on this, with more positive results. In fact, kiosks are just one type of customer-facing technology that is opening up new horizons in customer management. Retailers are beginning to consider the idea of leisure shopping inside their stores from wireless-linked terminals. These allow customers to see what is in stock without having to look at the shelves or rails. The increasing use of electronic systems by stores is leading to a world in which customers will be detected as soon as they are in the vicinity via a radio-transmitting loyalty card. Then, appropriate offers will be prepared for them and they will be offered a range of different ways to get through their weekly shopping.

DIRECT RESPONSE AND THEN INTERACTIVE TELEVISION

If experiments here succeed, the move to using this approach could be very fast, particularly given evidence that conventional Internet users are very frustrated with the time it takes to download files, which is even more marked if they contain moving images. Here, it is expected that cable modems and set-top boxes that contain Internet browsers will eventually become the norm.

Meanwhile, direct response TV (for more on this, see Bilton, K and Gofton, K, 1997, *A Guide to Broadcast Response*, Sitel) has become a key focus of the direct marketing industry and is seen as a crucial area for learning about likely patterns of behaviour as experience with digital interactive TV grows. In direct response TV, the classic direct marketing disciplines apply. These are:

▪ response handling, tracking and reporting;
▪ conversion tracking and so on;
▪ airtime accountability and media buying;
▪ forecasting response rates and cost per conversion.

MOBILE SERVICES

Services for people on the move (mobile computing, voice mail, messaging, mobile telephony and the like) have diffused rapidly and proved very beneficial. We expect this diffusion to continue and, slowly but surely, replace many of the static telephony functions, so that tracking down customers on the move or being tracked down by them becomes an increasingly important part of the mindset of database marketing, for both sales and service processes. We expect this to benefit visiting agents considerably as they should be able to sit down with the customer at work or at home and access any company information customers might require using mobile telephony systems rather than customers' own phone lines. Some organizations are introducing mobile satellite tracking to provide support to their customers. The RAC, for example, is working on a method of tracking accidents in order to speed up its response times to such incidents.

There may be a revolution on the way. In many countries, teenagers – among the most avid users of mobile phones – already ask the question 'Why should I be in a particular room to receive a phone call?' However, managerial customers have already answered the question 'Why should I be physically connected to anything in order to carry out any transaction or receive any information?' The vision mobile phone companies have is of each individual permanently connected to whatever they want to be connected to, but at low cost. This means that customers must be connected to a computer, not a person (except in cases where a computer can't do the job).

The interesting thing about the use of the new e-enabled mobile technology is that it provides excellent service at low cost to *all* customers, not just to a few premium customers. In fact, our vision of 'top vanilla' service (excellent service to all customers) is fast becoming a reality in some industries. Here are some examples:

▓ top airline customers – British Airways Gold members, for example – can be notified of delays to flights they are booked on, but Sonera, a Finnish mobile telephony operator, makes this information available to all mobile customers via a simple text message;

■ UPS, in some countries (the project is at pilot stage), allows all of its customers to receive a text mobile message for every scan of their packages, some being scanned as many as ten times from pick-up to delivery – this service is already available globally on the Internet, of course, and from other courier services;

■ Microstrategy in the US is building a complete business on e-content (www.strategy.com), in which the mode of delivery of the content is as the customer wants – Web or mobile.

The vision is clear – every customer, or perhaps only every validated customer, will be able to interact free of charge or at very low cost with their suppliers' systems (subject to appropriate security), reducing staff-based costs. This could be for anything – buying an insurance policy, viewing a bank balance, making transfers, checking the status of a complaint, finding out the progress of your car in the delivery or servicing process. Note that, in many respects, the mobile phone is the most secure device of all as it contains a powerful microprocessor and significant storage capacity, as well as several levels of security, enabling the use of much smarter customer validation techniques than is possible with a credit card.

Imagine, you have just bought a car and want an insurance quote or that you are considering buying one and want a loan or that you have just viewed a house and want to arrange a mortgage or that you're about to visit a store and want to know what happened to the last complaint you made or if the merchandise you ordered is in stock or that you're driving to the station and want to know whether or not the train you plan to catch is on time or that you're leaving the airport and the airport staff have just found your mislaid bag or that you're driving to the airport and want to know whether or not you're likely to get bumped off your flight. The vision is that you will use your mobile to log on and get the information you need or that you'll receive the message you need automatically.

Your suppliers will incur virtually no costs in supplying this kind of information, though they will have to set up the electronic facility. They may even reduce costs by contacting you quickly. However, will you accept this service from anyone? Of course not. In fact, the Web is already demonstrating that new media don't destroy old branding rules. Customers are more likely to develop this kind of information relationship with a company they know and trust. Product planning will become smarter, as data from today's requests from customers is used to determine tomorrow's offers – perhaps even today's as well.

If this vision is to become a reality, what must change in marketing and service? The obvious area for focus is on supply chain management, which in financial services companies is often as 'sticky' – slow, complicated, opaque – as it is in manufacturing. We believe we shall have to look to the most advanced European and South East Asian countries for early solutions. The relatively slow growth of mobile telephony in the US – caused by archaic tariffing practices – means that US financial services companies are starting with a disadvantage in this race. Some believe that the mobile Web race will be a more profitable one than the conventional Web race. This is simply because of the much greater diffusion of mobile telephony. The gap is expected to widen as mobile phone diffusion is growing faster than fixed Internet access in most countries.

What recommendations can we make to marketing and service managers about the mobile? At the moment, access via mobiles is becoming as cheap as land line access, but data transfer is relatively slow, which is why most product and service suppliers are focusing on services that can be made available via simple SMS text messaging or mobile e-mail. However, the forecasts are that this situation will have changed radically within two or three years. So, the recommendation is the old one – be there or be square. However, being there *today* is important mainly because of the need to learn how to do it, so that when it becomes the main medium for customer access (in three or four years' time), you know what you're doing.

There is another rather tougher implication. If you find that your call centres or customer service departments are drowned by calls from customers who give you no value during the call (such as when they are simply making balance enquiries) or at all because they are low-value customers anyway, that is because you have created this process. Most customers are not born unprofitable! Cost to serve is a key issue in customer management and is likely to become the prime justification for investment in mobile-based methods of customer service in the future.

CARDS, LOYALTY AND ALL THAT

Plastic cards – whether magnetic strip, optical or smart – provide examples of some of the best and worst practice in the use of IT in customer management. It is often hard to draw conclusions from this area that it is possible to generalize from because the technology is so closely associated with the product – some consumers might even describe it as actually being the product. We have already discussed in our work on CRM in banking some examples of leading-edge practices in using cards in financial services (Stone, M et al, 1997, *Retail Banking Customer Management*, Policy Publications). The practice leading charge card companies have of combining customer databases, good call centre practice and direct mail is hard to fault. The combination of an affinity group with a specialist credit card provider has also proved to be an excellent way of making profits from customer relationships for many companies (see Dungan, R, 1997, Affinity and beyond, *Direct Response*, 17 (5), pp 59–61). Where airlines are concerned, there is still some doubt as to whether or not all the effort that has been invested in similar areas is really paying off, as described in our work on the airline industry (Stone, M et al, 1997, *Targeting High Value Travellers*, Policy Publications and Stone, M et al, 1997, *Managing Frequent Traveller Schemes*, Policy Publications).

THE CUSTOMER DATABASE ITSELF

For a discipline born before the last war, it's surprising to find that most companies are still, metaphorically, in nappies, often with multiple, creaky databases. In the largest companies, the ones that work best are often not the newest, but, instead, based on mature, stable technology with proven scalability. One reason for this is that very new technology is often unstable and unproven. Also, some of the older customer database systems were designed with a single purpose in mind – mailing, for example. With several years of usage behind them, marketing and systems people have learnt to cope with the system and its foibles! However, in terms of the new requirements of marketing and service, these older systems are showing their weaknesses. The trouble often starts when the main data feeds come from such systems or when a marketing system is expected to share hardware with an operations system.

There is a view that marketing systems should run on their own boxes or else their needs will always be deferred when in competition with, for example, batch finance processes, such as invoicing or statements.

The hardware required to host customer databases has become much cheaper than it used to be and so now often forms a small part of the total budget for the new customer management approach. The ease of running such systems has been greatly enhanced by the availability of datamining tools that can be used off-line, reducing processing costs and times. However, as marketers find that analysing complicated customer histories going back several years can produce useful results, the processing requirements for the new customer marketing systems should not be underestimated.

Client/server architectures for customer databases are in vogue, but mainframes are coming back, as the need for integrated and companywide customer management systems and data is recognized. They provide industrial strength for databases that are being accessed from across the enterprise. However, communication elements of marketing and sales are becoming more user-definable and have less (although still significant) need nowadays for the controlled environments and expensive programmers that were the main drawbacks of mainframes. Also, many mainframe applications and fast-start tool sets are now available – data re-engineering tools and methods/skills, plus marketing database and ready-to-go data warehouse models, for example.

There is still little consensus about what a customer database is and how it should work. Many companies have spent great sums on failed customer databases or ones that underperform relative to their objective, are delivered late or with some functions that are unusable in practice. Our work on customer databases (Stone, M et al, 1998, *Relationship Marketing: The technology*, Policy Publications) shows much unclear thinking about the relationship between the database and its various applications, such as call centres, direct mail and customer service monitoring. Prospect data is often mishandled and even lost. There is much scope for improvement – using technology and improved processes.

Just as many companies have started to get on top of these problems, and move towards real customization and personalization of their offer, in the UK a new threat has emerged in the form of possibly more restrictive interpretation of data protection laws. This threat, as discussed in our work on customer management in utilities (Stone, M et al, 1997, *Managing Customer Service in Utilities*, Policy Publications), has been compounded by the likely introduction of slightly more restrictive laws based on the relevant EU directive. We believe that this pressure is based on a very narrow and uninformed view of customer service and marketing futures, which runs directly counter to the directions governments themselves are pursuing to target benefits more clearly and control fraud. The idea that only government should be allowed to manage certain aspects of their relationship with the electorate, eg tax payment or TV licence payment, but that companies should not be able to use it to identify customers who might be interested in their products and services, quite frankly, smacks of *1984.*

DATA WAREHOUSING, DECISION SCIENCE AND DATA ANALYSIS

Data warehousing is becoming more and more popular, although few companies have really adopted it fully. Its big advantage is that it allows companies to design their marketing and sales systems to be optimized for handling transactions and for the company's particular organizational structure. Then analysis issues can be resolved according to different sets of priorities – to provide customer management-based scorecards and profit models or identify particular groups of customers requiring different treatment across the enterprise, for example. Of course, data warehousing and datamining are not ends in themselves but, rather, should support the development of more competitive strategies or operations.

Datamining techniques and practices have evolved rapidly, with evidence of really strong gains, for example, in reducing unnecessary activities by ensuring mailings are targeted better and so on or achieving stronger focus on higher-value customers – especially higher future-value customers. However, there is still much to be done to make a more professional and rapid approach to quantification, analysis and subsequent action a stronger part of the marketing process, rather than something that is done afterwards to find out what worked.

Warehousing and then mining of customer data is most effective when it is enterprisewide, allowing the company to gain a single view of customer and business profitability. This contrasts with the approach often followed, in which only one aspect of a customer's relationship with the company is warehoused and mined – that aspect often being based on a particular organizational interpretation of the relationship, such as in relation to a single product.

Analysing data about customers over a long period can lead to a complete reinterpretation of a company's success or failure in managing customers. For example, what was seen as a problem in selling a new product might be seen as a problem of recruiting customers new to the category. It can also lead to quicker identification of where competitors are making inroads into your business, and also where new opportunities lie for your own competitive activity. (See our previous work on data warehousing, decision science and data analysis: Stone, M et al, 1997, *Effective Datamining*, Policy Publications.)

WHAT HAVE WE LEARNT FROM IMPLEMENTING NEW TECHNOLOGY?

Learning gained from these experiences includes the following.

■ Most customers do not really want to know about the details of new technologies, except, of course, customers who are themselves in IT departments! However, at the leading edge of an application, segmentation on ability to use a technology may be important so as to get enough users, cost-effectively.

■ Ideas are best and most cost-effectively driven forward by pilots and experiments as these quickly reveal what customers are prepared to do and want to do, where they want to change their habits and where they don't. They also quickly reveal where the technology really does improve things for customers. Even beyond the pilot or prototype, the implementation is more likely to be phased than a 'big bang'.

■ Companies often treat implementing a new technological approach to customer management as a technological experiment rather than a change to marketing and service technology. Even among productive users of call centre technology, for example, we find that it is not uncommon for senior marketing management to treat the call centre as a black box, although it is their main location for handling customers. This means that many opportunities for improving customer management are lost. For example, data on the types of customers calling and why they call are often not analysed for their implications for customer recruitment and retention.

■ The technology – in its various combinations – does change the relationship achieved. The best demonstration of this comes from the direct financial services providers and some utilities, which have succeeded in achieving an openness to customer contact that has directly improved their market share and customer retention.

■ Mass-customization is becoming possible. It is hard to achieve with physical products because the number of product dimensions that can be varied late in the supply process is difficult. Here, the best examples are achieved by automotive manufacturers, which have combined ideas of modularity with factory and supplier-facing IT to allow the cost-effective manufacture of many variants. They also use customer-facing IT to allow customers to explore and then order from a much larger number of variants. Other examples of this include manufacturers of furniture (particularly of the fitted kind), but also fashion. Levi Strauss experimented with capturing consumers' measurements electronically and transmitting them to the factory, allowing individually tailored jeans to be produced at much less than the conventional cost of bespoke tailoring. However, this service was terminated because it had the effect of cannibalization of shop sales. However, in service industries – such as financial services – where, in principle, almost anything can be provided, the key is to manage the cost–benefit and risk–reward profiles for both parties. The deployment of improved customer-facing technology allows the capture of more customer data, producing more suggestions about the areas in which customers would like to be able to vary the service. It also allows the customized product to be offered back to customers without human intervention.

■ Improved knowledge of customers and prospects is allowing companies to reduce the costs and increase the effectiveness of managing customers. Contact media (mail, telephone, field sales) can be adjusted to find the most cost-effective combination for each customer. Improved understanding of customers allows the best prospects to be targeted for new products. This may produce quicker product launch cycles, as targeted media are used to communicate with the best prospects. The best example of this is the Range Rover Mk 2 – the first major automotive product to be launched entirely by means of targeted marketing.

▨ Increasing use of systems has exposed the slackness with which marketers often use terms such as 'customer', 'prospect', 'loyalty'. Customers have many kinds of relationships with the companies that supply them, so if they are to be managed according to these relationships, then they need to be clearly defined using criteria based on data that is actually available.

▨ As the ability to store and manipulate data increases, there has been a strong move away from 'snapshot' marketing, which is based on an understanding of customers as they are now, to 'curriculum marketing'. This is because the supplier has access to more data about customers' developments over time and about key events in customers' buying and overall lifecycles. For consumers, there are various family and buying cycles, while for businesses – particularly smaller businesses – the cycle of establishment and maturation is overlaid by various product-buying cycles.

▨ Benefits cited by suppliers are usually better customer knowledge, more precise knowledge of what levers to pull to improve customer recruitment, retention and development and improved profitability of individual marketing initiatives. For some, the technology has opened new ways of managing customers – that is, channels. However, this does not imply that ways of contacting customers will be increasingly direct, as the benefit has been across the board. For suppliers who achieve high degrees of personalization and customization, a major benefit has been an increase in customer loyalty because customers feel that they are being treated as individuals and like it.

▨ For customers, benefits are mainly improved access to information and ease with which they can contact and deal with their suppliers. Sometimes, the improved speed (for example, case processing cycle time in financial services) has led to much less stress and cost for users. For businesses' customers – who often tie up great resources in dealing with their suppliers – the much closer relationship can lead to significant cost reductions, such as less paper, quicker response times, lower inventory holdings and so on. Also, improving customers' ability to affect the relationship – even customize it – can put more control in the hands of customers and some of them like this. In particular, customers increasingly want to access their suppliers at times and in locations and ways that suit them rather than suppliers. For example, in some cases, they want to separate information-gathering from decision-making processes, finding out information at leisure over weekends.

WHAT THE FUTURE HOLDS

One of the most difficult questions an IT director is faced with is 'Will the future hold anything that is qualitatively different or will it be more of the same – faster, more comprehensive and so on?' Of course, the answer is that it will be both. However, in terms of what actually *works* at the interface with the customer, it is interesting that the companies with the best consumer ratings (often what we call the 'new breed directs'), tend to combine tried and tested technologies with innovative marketing and customer service approaches. They stay well away from the 'bleeding edge'. Companies that are involved at the bleeding edge of customer-facing technology often do so as a *substitute* for a genuinely customer-oriented marketing and service policy that delivers more profit for the company and higher satisfaction to customers. New customer-management technologies take a long time to diffuse and big new systems to support them are often in place for ten years or more, with perhaps a significant update every five years.

So, the real question for an IT director is not how fast to implement new technologies, but how to ensure that they are used to support genuine business initiatives that will lead to big improvements in customer management rather than technical experiments as a substitute for much-improved marketing and service strategies. Remember, new technology will only deliver CRM objectives if the benefit to customers is clear, and this means that the benefit must be better than the technology it replaced.

CONCLUSIONS

Once a company realizes that it needs to manage relationships with customers as well as sell products and services, a new set of marketing and IT models must be adopted.

13

The Future of e-CRM

THE EFFECTS OF E-BUSINESS

So far in this book, much of our emphasis has been on the interface between companies and customers. However, it is clear that the transformations being stimulated and enabled by e-business 'behind the scenes' are having an enormous effect on companies' ability to serve their customers – they are becoming quicker, better, cheaper. There have been great changes in this area, some of which are described below.

Growing e-confidence

Greater confidence in using e-business techniques has stimulated many companies to open up a much broader range of functions to customers. For example, companies are allowing customers to specify products, view progress in delivery and so on. This opening up reduces many costs (such as telephony), while improving customer service. The approach has also been very successful in dealing with the many internal customer–supplier relationships that exist in large organizations. In some extreme cases, a company might decide that it is better off formally split-ting up the organization and selling off certain internal customer or supplier units, such as billing operations, manufacturing, inventory management.

The easier this becomes, the more important it is for companies to develop a view of their core competencies (see Figure 13.1). In some cases, this proves to be just knowledge! This is because wherever there is a process, it can be outsourced to specialists in that process. If this happens more often, it will expose those companies whose processes are slow or of poor quality. The advantage may go to companies that have focused on developing rule-based processes, particularly for formerly people-intensive functions, with escalation processes being referred to people only where necessary.

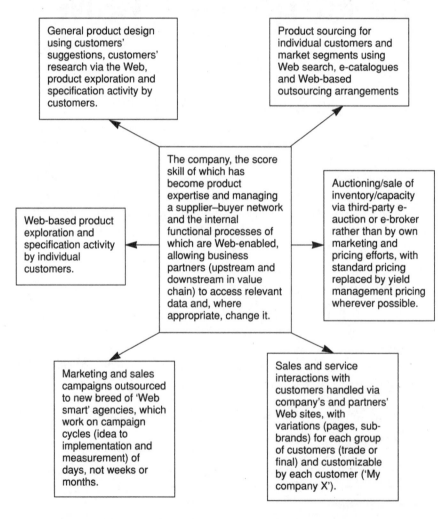

Figure 13.1 *The Web-based company – a possible future*

Emerging patterns of use and service

Much of the emphasis on how the Web is used focuses on the infinite variety of products and services that can be bought on it and the infinite variety of activities that can be conducted on it. However, in other respects the Web is starting to look like just another medium. A report by Media Matrix for the *Los Angeles Times* published in August 1999 showed that actual diversity on the Web was shrinking, with the 50 per cent of the most popular sites accounting for 35 per cent of Web usage, up from 27 per cent a year before, with the top 10 sites at 19 per cent, up from 16 per cent a year before. This excludes AOL's proprietary network – its 17 million members spend 75 per cent of their total surfing time within the proprietary AOL world, and one survey estimated that AOL alone accounts for 40 per cent of all American on-line activity. Yahoo! is trying to emulate AOL's success.

Search engines are decreasingly able to cope with the huge quantity of on-line content, much of it irrelevant to what users are searching for, although new second generation search engines, such as Looksmart and GoTo.com, are helping to deal with this. Users are therefore turning to sites that they know contain what they want, and attracting users to these sites is increasingly done by so-called 'off-line' advertising. So, C-Net announced in mid-1999 that it would spend US$ 100 million over the following 18 months to build its brand. Similar money is being spent by specialist sites such as www.monster.com (for jobs) and WebMD (for health). These high-spending sites need to make as much of their users as possible, so the focus is on adding services and content. Of course, some of the advertising is aimed at investors, to support or inflate the share price. However, much of it is also aimed at the seasonal market. For example, many US advertising agencies reported in mid-1999 that they were drowning in requests for media for autumn 1999 and had to turn advertising away because everything was already booked (see Hwang, S L, 1999, Web firms' ad blitz considers Wall Street, *Asian Wall Street Journal*, p 7).

Suppliers who go on the Web must realize that, when they do so, they are raising expectations of greater responsiveness and, in many cases, they are not lived up to. Jupiter Communications' 'Quarterly Customer Service Survey' shows that many Web sites take five or more days to respond to e-mails triggered by the site.

Travel sites have the quickest response times, but even their service levels are deteriorating. Financial sites and branded consumer goods have a much worse record. The shortage of Web-based customer service solutions is also indicted in the report. However, it also shows that customers' preference for live – as opposed to Web-based – customer service is still high in air travel and financial services, while books, music, consumer electronics and PC hardware and software are more receptive to e-service. *Datamonitor*'s July 1999 report on US on-line financial services supports this view, suggesting that while consumers may use the Web in increasing numbers for fact finding, they still require face-to-face contact and personal guidance for more complicated transactions such as auto finance and mortgages. However, this report also predicts that, for simpler marketing such as credit cards, direct mail will suffer at the expense of the Internet. This is because the latter now offers on-line approval of applications, while the direct mail channel requires a wait of several days.

Old-style approaches to understanding customers are now being adapted to the e-age. Engage Technologies of Massachusetts has a database with profile information on 30 million Web users, one third of all Americans who use the Web. The company tracks which sites individuals visit and how long they stay there to build a profile of interests. The profiles are then stripped of personal details and used for targeting. DoubleClick, an on-line profiling and advertising firm, recently announced its purchase of Abacus, a company that maintains America's largest database of mail-order purchasers. It expects its database on who clicks on what to name names (for more on this and other aspects of Internet data-gathering activities see *Time*, 2 August 1999, pp 40–3; for more on how companies are aiming to capture data on children, see pp 44–6, same issue).

Merger, acquisition, divestment and partnership

Continuing merger, acquisition and divestment activity in many sectors (oil, financial services, automotive, telecommunications, retailing, airlines and so on) has caused many companies to review their rather inflexible ideas in the area of IT strategy. They have realized that a once-for-all strategy of unifying in-company systems might make sense in a world in which no further corporate changes were anticipated, but not in one where mergers, acquisitions, divestments and partnerships seem to follow each other in an internal cycle. A more flexible e-model is emerging, in which interfaces between partners of all kinds are increasingly being handled using Web technology, while the information required to support these interfaces is imported into, and exported from, them to a variety of source systems using middleware. This approach also allows companies to avoid changing their source systems after each corporate change. This, in turn, allows them to develop or buy 'best of breed' systems for each business function (such as inventory management, billing, financial analysis), while ensuring that they deliver to each other and to the customer–supplier interface.

Corporate strategy change

The above example of corporate change is a special case of a more general phenomenon. In many markets, new competition, privatization, deregulation, disintermediation and reintermediation are causing firms to reappraise their strategies far more often. In these circumstances, it may make sense not to do as so many IT textbooks recommend, which is to develop IT strategy from corporate strategy. Instead, it may be better to focus on developing a set of core IT capabilities that are likely to be needed in a variety of strategic scenarios, using middleware to ensure integration in practice. It seems clear that, for most companies, e-capability is going to be a core capability, allowing improved customer service, lower costs and a greater ability to move fast to capture new opportunities.

It is this frequency of corporate change that is one of the reasons enterprise resource planning (ERP) software has experienced many implementation problems. Originally designed for comprehensive implementation within budget, Standish Group research shows that 90 per cent of ERP projects end up late or over budget. Only 20 per cent of ERP projects are single-vendor ones, 50 per cent have more than four vendors involved. This is because so many problems are encountered when integrating software with other systems that must be retained. A Gartner Group report in 1999 showed that ERP systems provide only 30 per cent of the functionality needed by businesses.

Activity acceleration, improvement and cost reduction

Various e-techniques, often coupled with creative use of middle-ware, have enabled companies to look at new ways of reducing costs and improving performance. One approach here is to reduce – or even abolish – any manual 'hand-offs' between processes, by ensuring that data flows smoothly between supplier and customer and within the supplier. Phrases such as 'supply-chain integration', 'straight-through processing' and 'zero latency' have taken a new and practical meaning for companies, as e-technology has allowed customer-driven and other changes to be implemented more quickly higher up or lower down the supply chain. For example, DHL's Connect Web site is built on messaging software from IBM.

Success of business-to-business trading

The Forrester Group has forecast a doubling of intercompany trade of goods over the Internet every year – from US$43 billion in 1998 to $1.3 trillion in 2003 – compared with consumer e-commerce – which is forecast to increase from $8 billion to $108 billion over the same period. The main industries that use it are computing and electronics, closely followed by aerospace, telecommunications and automotive and financial services, such as investment banking. The speed of progress depends on the ready availability of software, computing platforms and systems integration exper-tise. The current leaders are said to be Cisco, Dell, GE, Ford and Visa. These companies use the Web not only with customers but also suppliers, and downstream after sales. Ford's suppliers, for example, are told immediately each customer places an order.

An example of the wider benefits of such an approach is customer support. One way to reduce customer support costs is by allowing customers to post their own trouble-shooting knowledge on the company's system – meaning that, as sales grow, customer support costs decline as a percentage of revenue. If customer support skills are scarce, the Web enables expansion to take place that, otherwise, might not be possible.

In best practice companies, a high proportion of transactions take place without any human intervention. This also applies to internal customer–supplier relationships, such as those between cost centres and accounts, by putting expense management on the Web. Such practices have other benefits – quicker closing of accounts, allowing more rapid analysis to determine what needs changing, better cash flow management and the like. Suppliers can see how well their products are selling downstream of the business customer and, where they influence these sales (as at Safeway UK), they can react faster to any problems or opportunities. The difference between this and the old EDI approach is that the cost of connection to a customer's intranet is only a few thousand dollars, compared with millions for EDI.

This new approach to managing customers and suppliers can be described as 'turning the company inside-out'. Many activities that were carried out internally, invisible to customers and suppliers, are now carried out with high external visibility. Indeed, in a business-to-business situation where suppliers and customers are trusted partners, very little would be left invisible to customers or suppliers and very little would not be affected directly by them. For most companies, however, such an approach is a long way off. Despite aspirations to improve efficiency and speed via e-business and spread these gains to customers and suppliers, many companies still think of e-business as a Web site and so do not understand what the requirements are for major projects to deliver success.

To be used for e-commerce, a company's Web-based activity must support:

▓ customer database access and validation;
▓ on-line transactions – and, in the future, negotiation;
▓ access to suppliers' databases;
▓ integration with call centre operations;
▓ multiple payment methods.

A report by the Yankee Group in 1999 says that only about 20 per cent of large and medium US companies are anywhere near achieving the above. Making the change requires a cultural transition – seeing the company as an e-business hub. Customers and suppliers are invited deep into the organization and vice versa with their business partners. Trust is key.

The most frequently quoted example of a company having made this transition is Cisco, the manufacturer of Web equipment. It outsources all its manufacturing, having become an advanced intermediary between manufacturers and customers. The key aim of such a company is to make profit, but also keep its suppliers profitable and in touch so that they supply quickly and get paid quickly. Suppliers are also involved in upstream processes such as product design.

Eventually this approach will spread to services. For example, Home Depot is a do-it-yourself retailer whose Web site helps builders and consumers by giving them advice, and also helps builders find subcontractors. It helps them estimate quantities, provide supplies on time and saves wasted inventories for both parties. The classic advantages of a computerized value chain can now apply to small customers and suppliers, allowing the supply chain to work much more cheaply and quickly than was possible in the past. Auctioning can be used to clear any excess stocks. This approach may lead to the extension of yield management pricing way beyond its traditional domain of power supply, telecommunications and transport. In some sectors, automated yield management pricing will become the norm in automated purchasing. For example, Coca-Cola is testing machines that adjust pricing according to the weather. However, this approach does not destroy many of the central tenets of CRM as yield pricing can be adjusted to allow for individual customers' propensity to do more business, so the approach can be modified to attract good customers and retain them.

The rise of the infomediary

One of the main areas of interest to companies is how e-business can help them intermediate, disintermediate or reintermediate. In markets where intermediaries make high charges or cause cash flow delays, such as travel, Web-based services, whether by agents or suppliers, such as low-cost airlines, are proving very successful. In some cases, the Web encourages the different participants in the value chain to jump stages. For example, in a two-tier distribution system, with both wholesalers and retailers, end customers can buy from wholesalers and retailers from product suppliers. Some suppliers, such as airlines, have made the mistake of thinking that their best interest is served by taking on the whole system – for example, by going direct, rather than by encouraging strong intertier competition, so that distribution margins fall.

One of the great myths of e-business is that it necessarily favours direct supply to customers – whether business customers or end consumers. In fact, it is now quite clear that this is not so. One of the real strengths of the e-business approach is that it enables the break-up of within-company value chains so that one part of the company intermediates the sale of another part. It also allows the emergence of all kinds of Web-based intermediaries. Let us look at some examples.

In the US, the National Transportation Exchange (NTE) matches loads with empty trucks, creating a spot market for loads. NTE collects commission based on the value of each deal, the fleet manager or owner-driver gets extra revenue and the shipper gets a good price. NTE was originally set up on a proprietary network, but this was expensive and limited access only to those buyers and sellers prepared to invest. Similar intermediaries have emerged in a variety of businesses that have spare capacity.

This also applies within the marketing industry. For example, Adauction.com sells off spare on-line advertising space. There are three different types of auction – MarketPlace for a monthly auction, Tune-in for specific product categories and LastCall for last-minute sales. There are over 3000 registered buyers who have all undergone a credit check. Even a site as popular as Yahoo! can be left with over three-quarters of its advertising space unused. Adauction.com has now been relaunched as a vertical market portal (vortal), with on-line research tools and features such as news and discussion groups.

Chemdex is a similar Web site for research chemists, with nearly 200 suppliers offering nearly 0.5 million lab products. This saves users ploughing through lots of catalogues and spending a lot of time on the phone. Chemdex also uses procurement software to enable buying on the Web via the customers' corporate purchasing policy.

The above are examples of different infomediary roles. Chemdex is an aggregation role, compared with the auctioning role of Adauction and the broker/exchange role of NTE. However, all three could be combined on one site. Such approaches favour situations in which buyers and sellers are widely dispersed, where there is the lack of a real (as opposed to a virtual) marketplace and also where there is no single dominant company. Because of the knowledge and expertise needed to develop and run such sites and the willingness of commercial users to pay fees to get real savings, these types of sites are likely to be much more profitable than consumer sites. The share of business of these infomediaries is expected to grow rapidly. They have the economic advantage of balancing the power of buyers and sellers, letting neither dominate. They reduce the costs of switching for customers, but also those of finding new customers for suppliers. They allow customers to provide information on suppliers and suppliers to validate customers. They also allow small companies to get the advantages of big companies' systems, such as airline ticketing and billing. It seems that business-to-business infomediaries are most likely to succeed when they focus on particular opportunities.

So, this is not disintermediation, but just a new form of intermediation. Despite all this, there is still physical work to be done, but it can now be separated from commercial work. For example, infomediaries can match up buyers and sellers, but the suppliers' inventory managers and contracted physical distributors make the goods available and transfer goods. Of course, in same cases, inventory can be abolished altogether.

Some conventional intermediaries have moved to the Web. Marshall in the US and RS Components in the UK – both distributors of electronic components – now use the Web to serve tens of thousands of customers with products, information and support, and provide usage data to suppliers. Wyle Electronics Trading (semiconductors and computer systems) uses IBM middleware to link Web-based applications with mainframe-based corporate databases and warehouse systems. This means that when customers place an order on its Web site (www.wyle.com), nobody has to check it or rekey it.

DIFFERENT MODELS OF E-BUSINESS

In Chapter 2, we investigated a number of models of customer management:

■ **one to one** in which the company gathers lots of data about the individual and tries to adapt its entire offer as closely as possible to the individual customer's needs;
■ **transparent marketing** in which the company gives as much control of the offer as possible to the customer;

- **classic CRM** in which customer data is used to group customers to allow them to be managed in a limited number of segments with significantly different offers for each segment;
- **personalized communication and targeting** in which the offer is similar for all customers, but modified slightly to allow basic personalization and targeted appropriately;
- **top vanilla** in which a 'best of breed' offer is made to all customers, often combined with CRM for the most valuable segments;
- **pure spot-selling** on the basis of best value at the time;
- **spot-selling within a managed roster** in which the company focuses on getting on to the customer's roster and then offering best value;
- **spot-selling via an agent** in which it is recognized that agents make choices on behalf of the customer, so the aim is to get on to the agent's roster, if they have one, and then deliver best value;
- **channel partnership** in which the company works with channels to create and manage relationships.

Most of these models are facilitated by the e-business approach (see Figure 13.2).

However, as our discussion above suggests, we can now see companies emerging that trade using these models – often several at a time. One of the central questions confronting companies – as a threat and/or an opportunity – is 'What will be the role of the e-brand in my sector?'

The e-brand is one dedicated purely to e-business, targeting established brands doing business in old ways, aiming to slash costs. The above question is already being answered by the appearance of new types of companies, some of them acting entirely as e-brands.

The e-brokers

These are intermediaries who exist because they can link customers and suppliers more cost-effectively than other individuals or companies. In some cases, they can do this only because they are more specialized than others – whether in terms of products, marketing, delivery or service. Their suppliers can then focus more on their core business of producing the right products and

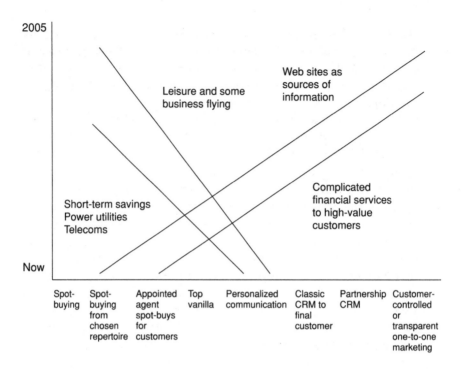

Figure 13.2 *How e-business is causing the sands of customer management to shift the dominant model of customer management*

keeping up an inventory of it. By maintaining links with different suppliers, an e-broker can often identify the best price for a given product or the most available product or the one that best suits the customer. However, this relies on some degree of commoditization of the product, such as its comparability in terms of standard features. If the product is a physical one, an e-broker arranges shipment via a specialist third party, such as a courier. Security between customers, e-brokers and suppliers is obtained by using electronic security measures.

One of the issues involved in being a broker is the sheer volume of trading that may occur – often in peaks. E-Trade has experienced problems when stock market trading surges, and this has led to potential legal problems as clients suffer losses as a result of their inability to trade. For this reason, Charles Schwab uses IBM WebSphere, which is scalable to cope with unknown demand. Schwab has about two million accounts and 50 per cent of its brokerage business is on-line.

A broker may work on any of the models, but is likely to do most profitable business by specializing and creating relationships with buyers so that the broker's service is best at meeting their particular needs. This is a combination of spot-buying and CRM/one-to-one models.

The manufacturer

Typically with configurable, modular products, a company's customers can build their own products by customizing with a click – as is possible with Cisco and some car companies. Pricing, finance terms, delivery and other related parts of the offer are also chosen by customers from an options list. By investigating the options customers try out, the company can get ideas about its future products, but also which features of its existing products are most wanted. However, this model can also result in the company realizing that its expertise lies in the assembly of customized modules, so it may also lead to outsourcing of upstream work in the value chain. The manufacturer effectively becomes an e-assembler, and in some ways echoes the functions of a value-added reseller.

Auctioning

Here, customers submit bids for products or services – possibly those that are not sold at standard prices, such as spare airline seats or hotel rooms. The auctioning company does not host inventory (as airline booking systems do), but extracts from them, charging a small fee to suppliers when a booking is confirmed. On-line auctions create wider, deeper markets, not dependent on people getting to an auction room. This leads to an increase in the price of certain assets, such as secondhand goods.

So far, much of the auctioning on the Web is simple – products and services are offered and customers can bid, using various rules. On eBay, auctions are transparent, so everyone can see what has been bid and bought, though this increases the risk of collusion, because participants can e-mail each other and negotiate side-deals. To control seller fraud, eBay allows regular sellers to establish reputations for quality and reliability by allowing buyers to comment.

Business-to-business auctions are growing rapidly and some commentators expect that they will soon constitute most of the volume, for example, of materials and components. Freemarkets in the US held auctions worth over $1 billion in 1998. This approach may spread into government areas, such as radio and other kinds of licensed work. E-STEEL is a steel exchange in which buyers and sellers bid for stocks of various kinds of steel. Many of these business-to-business sites are two-way auctions, in which buyers and sellers submit prices until matches are found, just like a stock market. The number of business auction sites in the US is over 500 and growing rapidly towards what is expected to be the several thousand mark.

New software will be required to emulate the full complexity of a buyer–seller market, particularly where price is not the only thing that is negotiated. IBM's research staff are already working on such software. The system schedules and advertises the auction, qualifies and registers buyers and sellers, sets up credit terms, accepts bids, informs the participants of the current bid situation, closes sales and settles payment and delivery schedules. It also integrates successful transactions with the company's back-office systems (see 1999, *Think Research*, (1), IBM).

One issue companies face is which auction model is best for which market. Dutch auctions – where the seller works downwards from a starting price until bidders bite – are good for liquidating inventory, while open-cry auctions – where bidders bid up the price – work best for single or limited numbers of items. Reverse auctions are also possible – where buyers tell sellers what they want and ask suppliers to bid for their business, which is a version of the classical industrial tendering situation. IBM researchers are also looking at situations in which buyers and sellers agree a price and then negotiate terms, such as delivery, payment schedule and so on.

Even in situations where formal auctioning is absent, it is now possible, using IBM technology (developed for the Japanese TabiCan project), to send electronic agents out to a variety of sites. These agents sit on the sites and watch them for best prices, e-mailing customers when a good price is found. Initially this is being developed for agents, but may eventually be released to final customers.

Of course, initially, users of on-line auctions are likely to be a biased group – focusing on price more than any other variable. However, this does not prevent companies from offering services to match higher prices. In fact, as experience in the travel market has already shown, customers often bid prices up above normal off-peak prices because they want a particular flight or a particular hotel on a particular weekend. In other words, setting just a peak and an off-peak price is an inefficient way to obtain higher revenues.

Making each model work

Each of these models has its characteristic workflow and systems support requirements, including validation of payment from third parties (typically banks). Today, a number of suppliers are offering complete software and even services, allowing companies to adopt different business models for trading on the Net (see Jutla, D et al, 1999, Making business sense of e-commerce, *Computer*, pp 67–75). For example, Made2Manage Systems has Web-based software for running an entire company's operations on the Web, designed specifically for smaller firms.

BROADER SYSTEMS AND MANAGEMENT ISSUES

Many companies assumed that having a single system to manage customers (often called a CRM system) or a customer database or a call centre was all that was needed. In fact, managing customers is a new discipline that often conflicts with existing disciplines. It not only requires different data, but also different decision-making processes, skills and incentives. Further, the discipline is changing rapidly with the introduction of e-business techniques and it will continue to change.

Therefore, many companies have now recognized that transforming customer management is a long and never-ending journey. Here, two- and three-year planning horizons are common – with different systems being gradually introduced to support the steadily improving customer management process – and clever systems integration work ensuring that the different systems talk to each other in real time.

Where customer management via the Web is concerned, the skills are scarce, as this involves blending CRM and Web skills. One of the major weaknesses in companies is the quality of their analysis and planning of customer management. In general, companies have poor knowledge of where they are and use their data on customers poorly to extract conclusions about which customers they are likely to obtain more value from, keep and so on. When the e-approach is introduced, life gets even more difficult and there is a need for a stronger foundation. This is because, as the e-approach generally passes more control to outside the organization, customer (and supplier) behaviour may start to change in unanticipated ways – and faster. This implies the need for smarter systems and processes to manage customers – or allow them to manage themselves. Without these, customers, suppliers and companies will probably not receive the benefits of e-commerce. This applies particularly when it is running alongside established ways of doing business, such as channels of distribution.

WHERE TO NEXT WITH E-BUSINESS IN CUSTOMER MANAGEMENT?

The informed customer

In many areas of customer management, the exchange of information has traditionally been a key to good relationships with customers. As we have seen in many of the examples above, customers' involvement in becoming informed is made dramatically easier by the Web. This is the more so in areas where customers have traditionally been deprived of relevant information by experts, such as in the area of health.

In the business-to-business market – always so receptive to improved information – we can see the new modes of business of broking and auctioning simply as extensions of information. Knowing what is available where, what companies want to obtain, what customers want to pay is all part of the freeing up of mutual access that conventional channels of communication and distribution have made 'sticky'.

The entitled customer

Governments have similar problems in managing large numbers of taxpayers. In Germany, legislation on digital signatures, public key infrastructure technology and consolidation of the financial and payments industries have created an environment ripe for e-commerce. In Spain, Spanish taxpayers can send their tax returns with digital signatures after using the tax return software (PADRE) provided to them via the tax collection agency's Web site (www.aeat.es). The digital certificate is installed in the Web navigator of users' PCs and issued by the Spanish certification authority Fabrica de Moneda e Timbre. It permits the Public Agency for Tax Management to verify and decode the relevant data.

Here, customers are being given the right to transact efficiently with government, not stand in queues, wait for telephone replies, fill in forms and the whole panoply of bureaucracy that governments are so expert at generating. This will have particular consequences for less developed countries, where state bureaucracies have always been a prime way of maintaining employment.

Making it easy to pay

After a faltering start, the world of electronic payment has arrived. Once again, business-to-business transactions have led the way, but we are now seeing more significant developments. For example, the Stuttgart-based electronic payment services company TeleCash provides a complete range of services for electronic cash payments, including debit, credit and pre-paid card transactions. It has installed around 125,000 point-of-sale terminals and generated revenues of $80 million in 1998. It offers public key infrastructure services to financial institutions, government organizations and corporate enterprises.

AN E-CRM CHECKLIST

Here is a checklist of some of the key issues and questions that need to be resolved as you implement e-business and e-CRM in your company.

Customer- and supplier-facing Web site and/or page design

■ Which Web sites and/or pages need to encourage intensive, prolonged use and which ones rapid visits? Does their performance match these objectives?

■ If your aim is to attract repeat visits, can you reduce the time taken for customers to re-identify themselves?

■ To what extent do customers want control of the on-line experience, in terms of its speed and functionality? How does this vary by segment or customer type? Do you provide this degree of control?

■ Is it important to allow your customers to customize the site to their own needs or collaborate with you in other ways? What benefits does this bring – to your customers, suppliers and you? Which aspects/functionality are most appropriate for this? How can customers be motivated to collaborate?

■ How does your performance compare with that of your competitors? How is your relative performance changing? Are there opportunities still left to be captured?

■ Have you provided incentives for potential customers and suppliers to register – gifts, requirement for purchasing, customization of information or service, extra functionality, privacy promise?

■ Have you investigated partnerships with other relevant companies? If you have taken this idea up, is your approach integrated with theirs rather than confusing – by allowing speedy links back to other relevant parts of your site, for example?

■ Does your site allow tracking of anything, where relevant, and does it allow push technology so that your customer does not have to keep logging on?

■ Does your approach facilitate recommendation of other customers and suppliers?

Customer loyalty and relationships

■ Does your approach recognize that e-business can make it easier for your customers to switch to or from you and for your suppliers to find other customers? Have you built in incentives for good customers to stay and give you more of their business and for good suppliers to give you preferred service?

■ Does your approach make it clear to customers and suppliers what your reasons are for wanting to deal with them in certain ways and the benefits they obtain from fitting in with your plans?

■ Do you continue to seek ways to give customers and suppliers control over the content, look and feel of your approach, subject to it meeting your objectives? This may include maintenance of personal profiles and preferences, choice of outbound and inbound channels of communication, service preferences in relation to delivery, billing and so on, choice of registration methods, choice of ways of receiving information alerts, sorting of any data presented during any interaction.

■ Do you use stored data to anticipate needs of customers and suppliers?

■ Do you use stored data to recognize returning customers and suppliers, making transactions easier, faster and more secure?

■ Do you allow visualization – that is, customers' and suppliers' exploration of how completing transactions or deepening relationships may help them achieve benefits, reduce costs, be more satisfied?

■ Does your approach allow customers and suppliers to communicate with others about the experience of doing business with you, your products and services, and how to develop better mutual value?

■ Is retention built into your products, pricing and communication, and can customers contribute to these in ways that make them more likely to stay (for example, by specifying contractual terms that suit both of you more)?

■ Does your approach make disloyalty a problem for your customers?

■ Can customers choose how to add value in ways that encourage them to stay? This may be by tailoring products or services to their needs, allowing them to give information at the right time, ensuring rapid reaction to information given, selecting small add-ons of high perceived value to them but low cost to serve for you.

■ Are there ways you can ethically make disloyalty inconvenient – by, for example, rewarding frequent use of the site and making infrequent use less convenient?

■ Have you identified the many different ways customers and suppliers can differ from each other and built into your approach the types of modularity that will allow customers and suppliers to adjust your approach to their needs while still enabling you to meet your objectives?

■ Have you investigated the different ways in which you can make your approach especially convenient to your best customers and suppliers – for example, by creation of privileged processes/pages for your best customers? Note that a precondition of this is that you have determined that it is better to discriminate between customers and that you can do so in practice.

■ Have you considered how interaction between your customer database and your e-business approach can allow acceleration of customer identification and meeting customers' needs, in all stages of the relationship cycle?

■ Does your approach recognize the same individual with several profiles, such as leisure/business, different degrees of urgency at different times or in different situations, different interest levels?

■ Does your approach incorporate drip irrigation – by gradual collection of data rather than one big hit, for example – then build by suggestions, by collecting data on different occasions, such as when ordering, customer service, tracking? Have you minimized the questions asked to satisfy customers' needs?

■ Does your approach allow inference – for example, by comparing the preferences of similar customers and suppliers – especially where preferences are given by example rather than explicitly?

Efficiency

■ Does your approach encourage straight-through processing, with the minimum of human intervention, whether in executing transactions or providing information? Where customers and suppliers might wish it, do you allow them to take on more of the work involved in transactions and the associated documentation, to mutual benefit?

■ Have you carried out 'cost to serve' and 'cost to manage' analyses of customers and suppliers and identified ways to reduce costs by accelerating, reducing or abolishing activities?

▮ Does the approach allow you and your customers and suppliers to bring information together from a variety of internal and external sources so as to allow them all to interact with you more efficiently and to meet their needs better?

▮ Is response to non-routine communications as automated and as fast as possible? Do you try to get customers and suppliers to use structured Web forms for this?

▮ Are push communications used where appropriate? Do you ask your suppliers and customers to incorporate this approach into their relationships with you?

Analysis

▮ Does your approach allow you to develop a clear picture, from all the data sets used in e-business (customers, products, market intelligence, customer contacts, forecasting, inventory and so on) of how customers' needs are changing and how you can adapt your approach to meet new needs?

▮ Have you built analysis acceleration into your approach, so you will understand how to improve your situation with customers and suppliers faster than your competitors?

▮ Is self-adjustment built in – that is, so that your approach learns and improves itself?

▮ Does your approach include a customizable, searchable knowledge base – general and customer-specific or supplier-specific frequently asked questions (FAQs), for example – allowing customers and suppliers to obtain quicker and more complete answers to their questions?

Interconnection and process change

▮ Does your approach allow your staff, customers and suppliers access to all relevant data sets and sources, such as other Web sites, inventory systems, logistics systems, call centres, scanned correspondence, back-office systems, complaints systems, point of sale, various data marts, campaign management systems, invoicing systems?

▮ Has your approach fully exploited the possibilities of merging, abolishing or accelerating processes and sub-processes – whether information management, internal activities or market activities?

▇ Have you identified what your core competences are in the electronic world – in particular, the extent to which they are based on rapidly renewing or changing knowledge and skills? In the latter case, do you have processes for ensuring rapid renewal or change?

▇ Have you identified processes that you are carrying out that are not best suited to your core competences and could be better carried out by customers and/or suppliers or by existing or possibly newly created agents or intermediaries?

Privacy, security and risk

▇ Have you taken appropriate steps to ensure the privacy and security of your customers and suppliers, explained to customers how you do this and what they need to do to maximize their protection?

▇ Do you give any guarantees in the areas of security and privacy, such as membership of third-party privacy organizations, such as TRUSTe, BBB OnLine? Is this possible?

▇ Where customers and suppliers may want it, do you allow them to explore your Web sites confidentially?

▇ Have you identified how and where your approach is vulnerable to bad customers and suppliers, and how customers and suppliers who are currently good might be motivated to turn bad by exposures that exist within your approach?

14

CRM Programme Planning

In our work over the last 15 years, we have identified the following basic models of project planning for implementing CRM.

- **Big bang** moving as rapidly as possible to implement CRM principles across the business. This, in general, only works for 'green field' businesses, those where there are no existing practices. It is very rare and normally only works in direct-only businesses, where strong central control can be used to ensure implementation. Even many direct-only businesses are product-oriented and have not succeeded in implementing customer management as they planned.
- **Steady progress** moving steadily towards a CRM vision, while recognizing that the vision will continue to change. For larger companies, often with a background of several CRM initiatives (some succeeding, some not) and usually a mixed history of relationships between marketing and IT people (especially in the area of data warehousing projects), this is usually the better option. However, it requires very strong project management disciplines as a series of projects are rolled out across the business, often starting with pilots to establish possibilities, capabilities and so on before rolling out CRM activity to the rest of the business. It also requires that some tough choices be made about where to start and where not to

and, indeed, whether or not parts of the business should be left untouched.

The 'steady progress' model is best visualized as a multidimensional diagram. Figure 14.1 demonstrates the situation in which only two dimensions are shown – in this case business units/products and customer value group.

		Business units/products				
		A	B	C	D	E
Customer group	Current high-value customers					
	Future high-value customers					
	Other customers					

Figure 14.1 *The steady progress programme model*

A key decision facing the company is how to combine breadth (doing something 'partial' across the business) and depth (doing something 'comprehensive' in part of the business). These terms are, of course, all relative – the essence of change management! In order to define these terms, we need to indicate the possible scope of change – that is, what other dimensions there are to CRM projects.

One set of dimensions relates to the business area or activity and includes:

▓ business unit;
▓ product;
▓ customer group, however defined – by need, value, growth, affiliation, behaviour, for example;
▓ geography, such as area or branch – this refers to the company's organization, not necessarily a geographical group of customers, which would be a customer group as below;
▓ function or other organizational subdivision, such as sales, customer service, claims, or department within a function, such as a call centre within customer service;
▓ communications channel, such as mail, outbound telemarketing;

▓ distribution channel – not only which channel to focus on, but also what level of channel, so that, for example, in an agent-managed channel, you would concentrate on agents rather than final customers;
▓ relationship stages, such as targeting, welcoming, cross- or up-selling, retention.

The scope can also be defined according to particular capabilities or enablers, often relating to infrastructure, such as:

▓ data, focusing on a subset of the data required for customer management;
▓ systems, focusing on some of the systems required for customer management, such as specific software, a new type of call centre;
▓ market research and analysis, focusing efforts, such as understanding customer profitability, future customer value and so on.

Although, in an ideal world, decisions on focus for the second group should be the outcome of decisions about the first group, in practice, issues such as feasibility and speed might dictate a compromise. Using these definitions, a breadth project could be customer retention across the business or targeting high- (current and/or future) value customers across the business. A depth project could be a complete change to the customer management approach for high-value customers in one channel for one product – that is, to include cross-selling of all other products.

Why is it so important to map out the programme in this way? Here are the main reasons:

▓ because the learning created as a CRM project that rolls across the company is highly transferable but takes time to arrive – rushing ahead means doing things without exploiting potential learning;
▓ the approach generates explicit attention to learning/knowledge management, ensuring that the relevance of lessons is identified and that relevant lessons are transferred quickly;
▓ the infrastructural requirement can be identified and planned more securely using this approach – in many companies, some

of the required systems' products and services have already been identified, but the direction in which the weapon is to be pointed has not;

▓ success generates a demonstration effect – rather than being asked to buy into change as an act of faith or based on business case analysis, managers can see the results;

▓ financial benefits arrive more securely, in line with the investment.

This approach should not be confused with the idea of 'low-hanging fruit'. In our experience, such fruit is sometimes left hanging low because no one wants to eat it. It is a mirage – it looks easy, but, on closer examination, proves to be very difficult. Cross-selling to an existing customer base is one such fruit. Many companies realize, after attempting this, that it has not been profitable. A common reason for this is that there is a poor match between ideal customer profiles and the products in question, perhaps they are bought at different life-stages.

However, cross-selling can be very successful if done properly – that is, when business intelligence is used to identify which existing customers are appropriate for cross-selling, in terms of life-stage, propensity to respond, need matching to product and so on. This success becomes a very positive first step in showing the value of business intelligence in helping companies understand their customers (and, implicitly, the cost of not using business intelligence). It all requires proper planning. However, it does not need to take a long time as most of the data comes from internal systems. Later, more sophistication can be added, such as giving financial data on customer profitability for each product. This increases the profitability of cross-selling.

Another key part of such programme planning methodology, as with all project planning, is that the inputs, outputs, accountabilities, timings, costs and benefits of each project and subproject should be clearly identified from the beginning. The approach is more secure but more complicated than the big bang approach because, rather than an extended period of preparation followed by implementation, many projects and subprojects require inputs from other projects and prove to be outputs to other projects over an extended period. An important implication of this project-planning methodology is that the projects started first are the ones that require the most significant changes, such as those to processes, systems, marketing strategies and so on, as it is usually these projects on which later ones depend. This is another reason for avoiding the temptation of low-hanging fruit.

In Table 14.1, we give suggestions as to projects and their definitions – including those where supply is via intermediaries or agents.

Only after a company's history of previous customer management projects, current and future marketing and strategic priorities, and organizational issues is understood can it be suggested:

▓ which products/divisions the pilot projects should apply to – though, in some cases, this will be obvious, such as retention needs to be applied where attrition is greatest;
▓ which dimensions should be used to restrict the scope of each project, other than those implicit in the title;
▓ the timings of each project;
▓ the interdependencies – because this can only be done when each project has been defined in detail, which also partly determines timings.

Note that Table 14.1 does not indicate the priority or order of projects. These are determined by the company's objectives and strategy, the urgency of getting a return on investment, its capabilities, its customers' or channels' needs and its market and competitive situation. In particular, our research shows that the availability and depth of information have an important influence. For example, predicting future customer or agent value in insurance requires historical data that may not be available or can only be made available with difficulty.

Table 14.1 *Some possible CRM projects*

Project name	Description/objectives
Good/bad agent definition	To define different good/bad agent profiles and categorize agents according to these profiles.
Good/bad customer definition	To define different good/bad customer profiles and categorize customers according to these profiles.

Table 14.1 *(contd)*

Future good agents	To develop profiles of agents whose forecast status is better than the present, and apply these profiles to the agent base.
Future good customers	To profile customers whose forecast status is better than the present, and apply these profiles to the customer base.
Customers of the future	To define how customers are likely to buy in the future, and what their needs will be.
Agents of the future	To define how agents are likely to work in the future, and what their needs will be.
Bad agent management/divorce	To profile agents whose current or forecast status is bad, and improve the status or divorce them.
Bad customer management/divorce	To profile customers whose current or forecast status is bad, and improve the status or divorce them.
Good agent winback	To identify good agents who have left and win them back.
Good customer winback	To identify good customers who have left and win them back.
Cost to serve	To identify individual customers or groups of customers where the cost to serve is too high, and reduce the cost.
Sales force management	To train, target, motivate and manage sales-force and their managers to achieve customer management objectives with agents.
Agent recruitment process	To make process of becoming an intermediary of the company best practice (speed, quality etc.)
Agent retention programme	To identify what makes agents stay and develop programme to improve retention.
Agent loyalty programme	To investigate whether or not agents would respond to a cost-effective loyalty approach eg tiered product/service availability.
Customer recruitment process	To make process of becoming a customer of the company best practice (speed, quality, etc.).
Customer retention programme	To identify what makes customers stay and develop programme to improve retention.
Customer loyalty programme	To investigate whether or not customers would respond to a cost-effective loyalty approach, eg tiered product/service availability.

Table 14.1 (contd)

Customer optimization/ cross-selling	To apply principles/software to ensure that the best customers are recruited and that cross-selling is targeted at the customers most likely to deliver value.
Customer attitudes/ preferences monitor	To identify whether or not customers will give information on attitudes/preferences and see whether or not this helps target customer management activities.
Agent attitude/preference monitor	To identify whether or not agents will give information on attitudes/preferences and see if this helps target customer management activities.
Customer details self-update	To identify whether or not customers will give key details – contact, life change – and see whether this helps target customer management activities.
Agent details self-update	To identify whether or not agents will give key details – contact, life change – and see whether this helps target customer management activities.
Lead management	To optimize the cost-effectiveness and quality of the process, with measures including future customer value.
Customer attrition prediction	To predict customers likely to leave or reduce commitment.
Agent attrition prediction	To predict agents likely to leave or reduce commitment.
Orphan management	To identify customers/prospects who are not being managed by agents and attempt to manage them towards us.
Pricing for future value	To identify whether or not pricing for future (eg retention) value improves overall profit.
Call centre welcoming	To optimize welcoming activities in call centres.
Call centre retention	To optimize retention activities in call centres.
Mail welcoming	To optimize mail welcoming activities.
Mail retention	To optimize mail retention activities.
e-mail customer management	To see whether or not e-mail can be used (more) cost-effectively to manage existing customers.

Table 14.1 *(contd)*

e-mail customer recruitment	To see whether or not e-mail can be used to recruit customers.
e-mail agent management	To see whether or not e-mail can be used (more) cost-effectively to manage existing agents.
e-mail agent recruitment	To see whether or not e-mail can be used to recruit agents.
Web customer management	To see whether or not the Web can be used (more) cost-effectively to manage existing customers.
Web customer recruitment	To see whether or not the Web can be used to recruit customers.
Web agent management	To see whether or not the Web can be used (more) cost-effectively to manage existing agents.
Web agent recruitment	To see whether or not the Web can be used to recruit agents.
Customer newsletter	To see how customer management principles can be applied profitably to customer newsletters.
Agent newsletter	To see how customer management principles can be applied profitably to agent newsletters.
Data strategy	To identify what data is required on customer/agent database and data warehouse, in terms of ability to generate profit.
Data quality	To identify where agent/customer data quality needs to be improved.
Customer operational database	To determine what customer data needs to be operationally available, eg in channels of communication/distribution, and how it should be made available.
Customer data warehouse	To determine what customer data needs to be available mainly for analysis.
Agent operational database	To determine what agent data needs to be operationally available, eg in channels of communication/distribution, and how it should be made available.
Agent data warehouse	To determine what agent data needs to be available mainly for analysis.

Table 14.1 *(contd)*

Integration of Web and/telephony integration	To see whether this is profitable and whether or not it enhances customer management possibilities.
Customer club/affinity	To see whether or not customers would respond to affinity programmes or a customer club.
Business partner programme	To identify whether or not there are existing or new business partners who would add value to the company's customer management approach.
Customer management product planning	To identify whether or not new products are needed which conform to customer management principles.

EPILOGUE: THE END OF A BEAUTIFUL RELATIONSHIP?

CRM has become a fashion, a menu for consultants to make money out of insecure companies. We sometimes refer to it as a 'Client Rip-off Menu'. It is an interesting recombination of tools and techniques – or as we refer to it, a Clever Repackaging Mechanism. As such, it is particularly vulnerable to the problem of 'guru guff' from academics and consultants who can only talk about their experiences as customers and may make incorrect inferences as to what the company was trying to do.

Making CRM work is most difficult when the business environment changes rapidly. Information technology has certainly had a radical effect here. Uncertainty is rife! Margins are threatened! There is no room for guru guff! This is particularly apparent in liberalized markets – particularly the utility, telecom and automotive markets. Relationships that were direct can become intermediated. Retailers now offer telecommunications services, contracting the supply either to the original providers or to small, fleet-footed 'new breed' operators, whom we access through our existing lines. The use of pre-paid mobile services means that the final customer is only known to the retailer (if they bother to ask) and not the network provider. Finally, the relationship is partially lost if we decide to opt for an alternative supplier through our existing line, in the sense that our line supplier no longer sees what we do. In the automotive market, brands will soon be available through all kinds of retailers.

So is this the end of relationship marketing? Of course not, but it does change the balance between CRM and classic retail and branded goods marketing. Some original product and service suppliers will focus on cost-effective manufacture, quality and, in some cases, strong branding, while the relationship is dominated – though not owned – by the retailer. In fact, consumers (perhaps using the Web) will decide with whom to have a relationship, and where it will sit on the spectrum between promotional continuity (usually based on rewards for buying more or more often) and true loyalty. They will do this not just according to what the relationship offers. They will, as consumers normally do, choose on whether manufacturers and retailers do their classic jobs: retailers to provide the right range in stock, at the right time and in the right place, and manufacturers to provide the brand, the image, the quality and reliability and, of course, the product. In this situation, one of the main roles of CRM will be to provide cost-effective and speedy ways to communicate these two propositions, and to create, enable and reinforce positive patterns of behaviour, such as getting the customer to buy. However, prudent marketing directors will always need to keep their eyes on whether CRM is the only – and the correct – model for their business.

Index